Geographies
of Difference

Intersections in Communications and Culture

Global Approaches and Transdisciplinary Perspectives

Cameron McCarthy and Angharad N. Valdivia
General Editors

Vol. 17

PETER LANG
New York • Washington, D.C./Baltimore • Bern
Frankfurt am Main • Berlin • Brussels • Vienna • Oxford

Edward Buendía & Nancy Ares

Geographies of Difference

The Social Production of the East Side, West Side, and Central City School

PETER LANG
New York • Washington, D.C./Baltimore • Bern
Frankfurt am Main • Berlin • Brussels • Vienna • Oxford

Library of Congress Cataloging-in-Publication Data

Buendía, Edward.
Geographies of difference: the social production of the east side,
west side, and central city school / Edward Buendía, Nancy Ares.
p. cm. — (Intersections in communications and culture:
global approaches and transdisciplinary perspectives; vol. 17)
Includes bibliographical references and index.
1. Segregation in education—United States. 2. Urban schools—
United States. I. Ares, Nancy. II. Title.
LC212.52.B84   371.829'00973—dc22   2006022455
ISBN 0-8204-8692-2
ISSN 1528-610X

Bibliographic information published by **Die Deutsche Bibliothek**.
Die Deutsche Bibliothek lists this publication in the "Deutsche
Nationalbibliografie"; detailed bibliographic data is available
on the Internet at http://dnb.ddb.de/.

Cover design by Lisa Barfield

The paper in this book meets the guidelines for permanence and durability
of the Committee on Production Guidelines for Book Longevity
of the Council of Library Resources.

© 2006 Peter Lang Publishing, Inc., New York
29 Broadway, New York, NY 10006
www.peterlang.com

All rights reserved.
Reprint or reproduction, even partially, in all forms such as microfilm,
xerography, microfiche, microcard, and offset strictly prohibited.

Printed in the United States of America

CONTENTS

ACKNOWLEDGMENTS vii
INTRODUCTION 1
    Framing Knowledge and Social Space 5
    A Word about Language 6
    Organization of the Book 7
1   DIVIDED CITIES, DIVIDED SCHOOLS,
    DIFFERENTIATED KNOWLEDGE 11
    The Apartheid Condition of City Space in the US 12
    The Production of Meanings of City Spaces 16
    Differentiated School Spaces 19
    Differentiated School Knowledge 20
    Institutional Construction of Student Identity 25
    The Landscape of Our Examination 27
2   KNOWLEDGE, THE PRACTICE OF DIFFERENCE,
    AND SOCIAL SPACE 28
    Knowledge 29
    Revisions to the Received View of Knowledge 31
    The Role of Practices and Technologies in Knowledge Production ... 36
    Space and Spatialized and Spatializing Practices 38
    Two Examples 39
    The Contingency of Knowledge Production 41
    Space, Knowledge, and Practice as Trialectically Constituted 42
    Space, Knowledge, and Practice 44
3   HISTORICAL FORMATION OF A GEOGRAPHICAL DIVIDE 45
    The Historical Landscape of the City 46
    Historical Practices of the West Side and East Side 51
    Contemporary Media Constructions of the
        West Side and East Side 54
    The Convergence of Discourse, Material Relations, and Practices 57
4   EAST SIDE/WEST SIDE: THE SPATIAL PRODUCTION
    OF DIFFERENTIATED STUDENTS AND SPACES 58
    We Are a West Side School with West Side Students 59
    We Are East Side Up Here 65
    Spatialized and Spatializing Technologies of East Side/West Side 69
    The Spatialized and Spatializing Reform 72
    Summary 76

5	THE CENTRAL CITY SCHOOLS: THE AMBIGUITIES OF	
	THE BORDERLANDS	77
	The Productive Nature of Teachers' and Principals' Discourse	78
	Constructing a New Discursive Code	79
	Dynamics that Spur Spatialization	84
	Spatialized and Spatializing Technologies of Central City	87
	Summary	90
6	THE DURABILITY AND FLUX OF LOCAL	
	SPATIAL KNOWLEDGE	92
	Spatiality of Institutional Knowledge	92
	The Knowledge of Difference and School Re-segregation	96
	The Active Production of Space	98
	Durability Through Reinstantiation	102
	Disjuncture and Contested Space	104
	Conclusion	106
APPENDIX	....	115
REFERENCES	....	119
INDEX	....	129

ACKNOWLEDGMENTS

The University of Utah's Department of Education, Culture and Society, and the University of Rochester's Warner School of Education and Human Development provided important support to each of us. They, particularly, provided us with time to focus on this work. We, of course, have many people to thank as well.

William Smith, Doug Hacker, and Andrew Gitlin were members of the research team that conducted the larger project. Their work helped push our thinking, as well as added insights only possible from an 'insider's' point of view. Numerous graduate research assistants were similarly intimately involved, especially Megan Peercy and Brenda Juarez, along with Chad Rhinehart, Lina Prenata, Dawn Evans, Al Schademan, Charise Nahm, Vianey Moreno, Francis McConaughy, Richard Garcia, Shane Koller, and Beverly Hacker.

The idea that conducting and publishing research is entering into a conversation is helpful in acknowledging others who have helped us along the way. Harvey Kantor, Frank Margonis, Donna Deyhle, Dolores Delgado Bernal, Norma Gonzalez, and Audrey Thompson read the manuscript closely, offering critical insights and challenging us in ways that pushed our thinking and helped us to clarify our arguments. Cameron McCarthy was critically important to our entering the conversation embodied in this series, shepherding us through as series editor. The intensive work of Sophie Appel and Damon Zucca at Peter Lang was greatly appreciated.

On a more personal note, Nancy Ares' family (Bob, Shane and Adrian Minckley) provided warm encouragement, and her parents, Charles and Jean Ares, read drafts of chapters, argued and praised. Ed Buendía's family—Sandra, Savina and Briana—was incredibly giving as weekends and evenings were consumed with writing and dinner chatter about this project.

Chapters four and five were initially published as: Buendía, E & Ares, N. (2004). Geographies of difference: The production of the East Side, West Side and Central City school. *American Educational Research Journal*, 41(4), 833-863. Reproduced with permission from the publisher.

INTRODUCTION

All major cities in the US, as well as most urban centers around the world, are marked by socially constructed boundaries that geographically divide areas along racial, ethnic, class, and, even, religious lines. Chicago has its South Side, New York has a racial and class division that splits Harlem from Manhattan. Houston, Boston and Toronto, to name a few other North American cities, all have similar spatial designations that mark certain places of the city as different than others. While terms such as the South Side or the West Side denote different geographical spaces, they also function as a local knowledge–with specific propositions of meaning–that defines the identity of individuals and groups who live in or come from these places. Historically, these different designations have come to mark for some inhabitants of these spaces a sense of collectivity, place, and belonging. For those who reside, or originate, elsewhere in these same urban centers, these constructs have functioned as a point of contradistinction, or as designations used to set oneself apart, from particular racial, class, or religious groups. They are deployed in a manner to denote, "That's them, not us." Hence, competing meanings may exist side by side within a city's representational framework where these codes signify pride and an affiliation with a cultural and community space as well as denote a pejorative assemblage of meanings that inscribe particular people and spaces with a sense of 'Other-ness.' Within many cities, spatial-ontological constructs such as these have been circulated and imprinted so profoundly in the imaginations and language frameworks of their citizenry that these designations are used as shorthand–as "the East Side" or "the South Side"–to name the unarticulated racial and classed markings of its inhabitants.

While the constructs of the East Side and the West Side are produced and sustained by city planners, politicians, the media and city inhabitants themselves, this book argues that these terms are more than just spatial signifiers that mark a place or an origin. We hold that they are codes underpinned by local knowledge, or what we will frame as discourse, that index racial and classed meanings of people as well as construct places within institutional and city spaces. We further argue and show how city educators are also involved in the production and maintenance of these codes and knowledge about city space and group identity. We argue that principals and teachers also actively participate in producing and sustaining these spatial constructs that inscribe students and spaces with particular encoded meanings of race and social class.

Contrary to arguments found in the educational literature that posit that educators solely inherit socially constructed classifications from their surroundings, this book puts forward the premise that educators are important producers of codes of difference within cities. These codes functioned in a double fashion, similar to the shorthand used by other city relations (i.e., media, politicians, residents). They, first, denoted specific meanings about race and class, specifically denotations that created hierarchies of those inclined and disinclined to education, as well as the civil and uncivil subject. Secondly, they also worked to obscure these meanings from public view so that institutions appeared, at one level, to be color- and class-blind. That is, educators, in this case, produced and employed an institutional knowledge of the "East Side," "West Side" and "Central City" student and school that affixed particular racial and class denoting meanings of differentiated intellectual capability, social experiences and aspirations between students from different areas of the city. Furthermore, educators deployed these constructs as codes that hid, for the most, any direct reference to race and social class. Such practices, we proffer, positioned educators as participants in the broader post-Brown (i.e., Brown vs. Topeka decision) project of obscuring explicit references to race and social class through the subtle codification of race and class, all the while that institutional practices signified clear references to these constructed subjectivities.

While arguing that spaces and students are enveloped by these codes, this books also argues that the institutional identity and work of educators in schools is entangled in this knowledge. It shows how teachers and principals framed their work and mission as different from other educators from other parts of the city. For example, teachers and administrators identified themselves, and were identified by others, as East Side, Central City or West Side schools and teachers. For educators from the city or region, these designations needed no further explanation. These terms indexed an understood knowledge base of spatial, historical, and ontological properties.

While these designations may appear on the surface as innocuous labels, this book argues that this knowledge has a great deal of force in coordinating bodies, practices and the material relations of schools and cities. The knowledge framework of the East Side, West Side and Central City school and student worked, we will argue, in tandem with school technologies in ways that configured them to function in concert with the meanings of spaces and populations. The effects, we will show, are entrenched compensatory discursive practices and educational programs for particular students, primarily immigrants and students of color, and enriched and varied programs for others, specifically white, middle-class students. Equally, spaces of difference were constructed such that students and teachers, as well as the spaces that they inhabited, were envisioned and treated differently. The long term implications of these relations and practices were the creation of technologies that had a centrifugal pull on new instructional technologies that were introduced into school settings so that they buttressed the existing logic of difference and further propelled the chasm that prohibited access to students who lived on what was deemed the "West Side" (i.e., immigrants and students of color) to high status knowledge and complex academic competencies.

This book of the West Side, East Side and Central City knowledge, student and school builds upon and contributes to the various works exploring how our world is socially constructed. While the argument of the socially constructed self/selves is not a new one (Foucault, 1978; Omi & Winant, 1991; Popkewitz, 1998A; Rose, 1999), educational researchers are finding that there is still much to be understood in comprehending the processes and apparatuses involved in such events of construction (McDermott, 1996; Popkewitz, 1998B). Particularly, we find ourselves needing to understand the way in which knowledge frameworks are connected to broad social relationships that interplay with and come to constitute, or make, educational spaces and subjects. Equally, we need to comprehend how the production of difference and marginality are maintained institutionally, particularly in ways that move beyond discussions of teachers' belief systems and expectations or structures of exclusion. The tools found in the field of sociology of knowledge are well suited for this task. Specifically, we locate this in what Nicholas Rose (1999) terms the sociology of power. By this, he is referring to a Foucauldian framing of practice and subjects as outcomes of matrices of knowledge and power. The knowledge and power exercised in producing the West Side, East Side and Central City schools and students will be the terrain that this book maps.

This examination of the social construction of East Side, West Side, and Central City schools and students takes place within one metropolitan school district, the Salt Valley School District (Western US). We analyze the meanings, uses, and production of these constructs by elementary teachers and principals within sixteen schools. Our aim was to understand the parameters of this knowledge, as well as its implications on practice. Specifically, we map the manner in which this knowledge works through and is co-produced by relations such as educators, the city's media, local politicians and institutional technologies to impose and to sustain these constructs upon bodies and objects. We show how the knowledge of the West Side, East Side and Central City comes to bear as educators engage in everyday pedagogical practice. We identify how this knowledge functions in doing the recognition work (Gee, 1999) of defining students' and schools' ontological properties (i.e., state of being) and, concomitantly, in functioning to name students' needs and designating the purposes of instructional technologies.

The description of the ongoing spatialization (Shields, 1997)–or social production of spatial subjects–as East Side, West Side and Central City schools, teachers, and students is also accompanied by our theorization of why this knowledge is so pervasive within schools. We read across the landscape of schools and their various social relationships (i.e., local, state and national) to explain why the race- and class-indexing knowledge of the East Side and the West Side are central constructs for educators within Salt Valley. Finally, we identify the implications for educators, students, and citywide residents when institutional agents (e.g., educators, politicians, media) invest professionally in this knowledge. This theorizing foregrounds the spatial (i.e., relational), historical, and institutional dimensions of school knowledge to explain its coherence as unquestioned institutional truths. Drawing from Nancy Fraser (1991), our argument follows that the relations that compose the space of schools, as well as the historical practices that have emerged as effects of these relationships, necessitate, in part, that educators produce these spatial categories. We posit that educators produce these as a means of responding to the legal and administrative mandates that are defined by the state and national level governments of attending to those seen as 'at-risk.' We show how the knowledge of the West Side, in particular, parallels the logic of the national discourse of 'at-risk' and, subsequently, provides educators with a framework of agency as they translate these state and national juridical and administrative edicts into spaces of therapy.

Yet, we argue that there is more to the production of this knowledge than just responding to the exigencies of state and national governing apparatuses. We forward the argument that the knowledge of the West Side and the East Side is also an effect of local historical discourses of white fear and local economic activity (i.e., development and consumption) aimed at rendering particular spaces desirable or undesirable. We argue that the institutional knowledge of the East Side and the West Side has to be seen in relationship to broader citywide discussions of "safe spaces" to live. The designations the East Side and the West Side function, we suggest, as codes for white residents to demarcate the desirable and less desirable places to live and, most importantly, to send their children to school. We interpret these processes as a local instantiation of the new symbolic language of the politics of race (Edsall & Edsall, 1992; Jacobs, 1998), where race is obscured through codes that subtly index local meanings of race. The city's real estate market as well as its processes of economic development are tied to the representations of space and people that circulate. These activities of naming and investing resources based on these distinctions propel a historical pattern of racial segregation in the city and its schools. We argue that these acts position educators within relationships and practices where schools become one more relation that produces and works from the racialized and classed discourse designating spaces and people of the city as the safe/unsafe and the desirable/undesirable.

Our theory that institutional knowledge is constructed in dialogue with broader city and national discussions places the emphasis of our project on the spatial, historical, and political dimensions of school knowledge. This focus lies in contradistinction to discussions of school knowledge as confined to disciplinary frameworks or personal beliefs (cf. Ahlstrand, Carlsson, Hartman, Magnusson, & Rannstrom, 1996; Bullough & Gitlin, 2001; Timmerman, 2004). In engaging in the analysis of the various data, the social and historical dimensions of institutional knowledge overrode the arguments that the knowledge of elementary educators was bound to personal or professional frameworks. The continuity between the knowledge of the West Side and East Side in spaces such as elementary schools and the statements of local politicians and the media compelled us to understand its emergence, its boundaries of discursive inclusion and exclusion, and its life in practice as a spatial, historical, and political relation.

Framing Knowledge and Social Space

A central premise underlying the work that we have undertaken here is that the knowledge of the East Side, West Side and Central City is discursive in nature. To talk about this knowledge as discourse, our analysis takes a poststructuralist turn to conceptualize these spatial markers as statements, or configurations of language, that cohere into semi-fixed institutional meanings and practices. Various discourses converge and overlap to create a system of reasoning that bounds what a person or collective can say and do within a particular set of relationships. In order to engage in our analysis we draw upon Michel Foucault's (1978) discussion of the institutionalization of discourse as knowledge. We seize upon the relationship that this line of thought establishes between knowledge, discourse, and practice to examine the social production of institutional knowledge, one in which knowledge and power are enacted as and through discourse. We also retain the emphasis that he places upon the historical, the institutional, and the embodied to present a narrative that shows how the West Side, East Side and the Central City subject and school are produced at the points of overlap between macro- and micro-relations.

At the same time, we also integrate Foucault's discussion with Henri Lefebvre's (1991) and Edward Soja's (1996) theorizing of the various relationships that come into play in these processes to produce space. It is in integrating these bodies of work where our analysis slips into a discussion of spatiality as products of knowledge, embodied practice, and material objects. The re-interjection of the material world, or what we will frame as technologies, is an important one. The poststructuralist turn towards language has dislodged the material world from many researchers' analyses as they have pursued understanding the language games that are both permitted and performed within particular contexts and situations (Clark, 1997; McLaren & Farahmandpur, 2000). What we proffer in this book is that it is not solely the realm of language that comes to bear in the construction of the entities of the East Side, Central City and West Side schools and students, but also the technologies that become part of the dispersion of social relations that institutionally produce and sustain such distinctions. Our aim is to show how "words and things," to borrow from Foucault (1972, p. 49), are involved in the ongoing social construction of school subjects (i.e., people), space, the ways of knowing, and of the imaginary (collective presuppositions about self and Other) of those who inhabit and work within schools.

A Word about Language

The written representation of the East Side, West Side and Central City construct found in this book is only one written form in which these constructs have manifested publicly in Salt Valley. These are socially constructed terms. At times, they are used in the media as the "westside," "West Side," or even in a hyphenated form with each word capitalized, as

"East-Side." They are not official designations that can be found on any map of the city. Furthermore, there is ambiguity as to where the boundaries of these spaces begin and end. Yet, all of these written forms of these spaces and inhabitants have appeared at some time in the city's newspapers, and are deployed by people to name themselves or others.

Organization of the Book

The organization of this book begins with a discussion of the different empirical conversations that situate our ensuing analysis and discussion. Specifically, in Chapter 1, *Divided Cities, Divided Schools and Differentiated Knowledge* we nest studies of cities, schools, and school knowledge in a way to show their inter-relationships. We provide readers with a reading of these relationships where racially and economically segregated cities have translated into segregated schools and differentiated distribution of knowledge across these schools. Structural analyses predominate within this literature on the racial and economic divisions within cities and schools. Most of this research has deemed the economic and social ecology of cities as the determining factors of schools' demographic and organizational patterns. However, other lines of research, specifically poststructural analyses, have challenged the structural determinism of structural analyses. We position some of the key poststructural analyses of schools in this conversation where knowledge, or representations of populations and city spaces, is also positioned as a tool of propelling division and differentiation.

Chapter 2, *Knowledge, the Practice of Difference, and Social Space*, describes the analytical terrain that we employ to ground our study of the knowledge of the East Side, West Side and Central City school, student and teacher. This involves an explanation and integration of the theories employed to pursue examining educational knowledge, the production of difference, and space. We describe Michel Foucault's revision to Enlightenment views of knowledge and his recasting of the concept as discourse, which he frames as formations of propositions that function to bound and order how an object can be envisioned and acted upon. Furthermore, we connect this theory of discourse to the material world by discussing how objects become technologies as they are integrated with discourse. Lastly, this chapter also argues that discourse and technologies are spatial and spatializing in their production, or located relationally and locating of other spatial relations. To describe these aspects pertaining to space, we define the conception of space with which we align our theorizing. It is here where Michel Foucault, Edward Soja and Henri Lefebvre converge.

The theoretical work that frames this analysis prompts us to identify the genealogy of knowledge formations of the city's spatial categories. The focus of Chapter 3, *Historical Formation of a Geographical Divide*, sets out to show this by tracing the historical emergence and social coordination of the knowledge and space of the East Side and the West Side within the city. We examine past and current local newspapers and other community based texts (i.e., position statements and speeches of local politicians) using a Critical Discourse Analysis (Gee, 1999) in order to identify the propositions that have been coupled to these constructs outside of schools. The chapter shows how the West Side construct has a history of signifying racialized discourses of "the criminal," "the dangerous," and "the undesirable" to describe the areas of the city where immigrants and migrants have resided. We also document how the specifics of the East Side construct have remained relatively invisible over time, but have surfaced as part of a binary (i.e., West Side/East Side) to give it some definition. We establish that there has been a great deal of coherence over time and across spatial relations in this knowledge by discussing the shared meanings of this knowledge in practices outside of schools.

In Chapter 4, *East Side/West Side: The Spatial Production of Differentiated Students and Spaces*, and Chapter 5, *The Central City Schools: The Ambiguities of the Borderlands*, the analysis turns to Salt Valley City's elementary schools to examine the institutional production of the spatio-ontological knowledge of the West Side and East Side. Chapter 4 describes the parameters of the knowledge of the West Side and East Side that is produced by educators who self-identify, and are identified by others within the school district, as West Side and East Side teachers and schools. In this chapter we show how the knowledge put into motion by educators proffered a line of reasoning of those from, and those inhabiting, the West Side as "deficit," "uninterested in education," and "at-risk." It identifies how this knowledge of the West Side was a racialized discourse of deficiency that, at times, explicitly named race and social class, and, at other moments, avoided identifying the racial identifiers, using instead the West Side signifier as a proxy to denote the racial dimensions of this knowledge. At the same time, we demonstrate how the construct and its deployment by educators propelled the coordination of material objects that spatialized these constructs at the level of material objects.

The analysis in this chapter also shows how the East Side construct was a marker that generally rendered race invisible. It demonstrates how it was coupled to propositions of the "enlightened," the "invested" and the "intellectually prepared" student and population in the few instances when it was elaborated upon. Its social life, however, was generally subdued in comparison to that of the West Side. We show, how it, too, was employed as a proxy to name and discuss race and class, as well as how it coordinated people and resources to produce a differentiated space called the East Side.

While the East Side and West Side binary dominated the knowledge base of most educators within this metropolitan school district, there was an element of complexity in the representational system of talking about the schools and students that composed the school district. In Chapter 5, *The Central City Schools: The Ambiguities of the Borderlands*, we describe a third space that existed in the division of schools and students in Salt Valley City District. It explains and theorizes the knowledge produced by 8 elementary schools that were situated spatially between the areas constructed as the East Side and the West Side. The schools in this corridor, or what we term and theorize as a borderland, identified themselves as not East Side or West Side. Instead, they identified themselves as constituting what they termed Central City. The chapter describes the different knowledges that educators summoned to talk about this space (i.e., people and things), the demographic shifts that have brought about this ambiguity in the knowledge of this space and its inhabitants, and the nature of these educators' mission as an effect of this unsettled knowledge. It shows and argues how this knowledge is a hybrid of local and national discourses. The local knowledge base was those that were found in both East Side and West Side schools, particularly nostalgic frameworks of educating that are prominent within East Side schools and at-risk discourses that are prevalent within West Side schools. The national discourses that were interwoven with the local meanings, on the other hand, were those national discussions about urban, at-risk schools.

Finally, Chapter 6, *The Durability and Flux of Local Spatial Knowledge*, discusses, at the level of theory, why these constructs are pervasive within spaces such as schools. This chapter takes up two central arguments to theorize the production and persistence of spatialized knowledge and difference. The first draws upon the theorizing of authors such as Nancy Fraser, Michel Foucault, and Tom Popkewitz to argue that the production and practice of this knowledge is inherent to the juridical, administrative and therapeutic inclinations of western institutions. The second dimension of our argument posits that the inclination to construct and govern differences is also enmeshed with local discourses of desirability and impulses to denote spaces of order and disorder. While school-based technologies position schools to make distinctions that produce the East Side and West Side student, school and teacher, the discursive practices of city politicians and the media work to locate spaces of violence and disorder, as well as their counterparts of safety and civility. When these relations discuss the East Side or the West Side, they are represented as racialized spaces, where the spaces of violence and disorder are denoted as Latino and Asian spaces. The safe, tranquil, and white spaces of the East Side remain invisibly racialized.

We hold that spaces and subjects are both constructed and reified. The city's institutions, such as its schools, also become involved in these processes as educators expand this knowledge as they deploy it to educate the West Side and East Side student. We close this analysis by extrapolating on the findings to argue that these educational practices also drive city and school re-segregation.

CHAPTER 1

DIVIDED CITIES, DIVIDED SCHOOLS, AND DIFFERENTIATED KNOWLEDGE

The relationship between differentiated city spaces and differential school experiences has been well documented over the last forty years. Various authors have presented the educational community with compelling analyses that contrast, or facilitate the comparison of, the educational conditions and experiences of inner-city Latina/o and African-American children with those of white students in suburban schools (cf. Kozol, 1994; Lipman, 2002; Orfield, 1996; Valenzuela, 1999). Many of these have provided us with structural analyses tracking the demographic patterns of white flight and capital (Kantor & Brenzel, 1993), the unequal allocation of financial resources (Kozol, 1994), and the disparities in programmatic (e.g., International Baccalaureate or Honors Programs) offerings between different neighborhoods (Lipman, 2002). In this chapter, we situate our examination by providing readers with an overview of these various discussions. Specifically, we begin by examining the various studies that have documented the patterns of organization of city spaces and the meanings, or representations, associated with these different spaces. This literature is an important backdrop in helping us to contextualize educational processes to a broader social geography of people, places and knowledge. We then couple this to educational discussions that have tracked the segregation of people and knowledge. The central thread that we follow in examining this literature is how the relationship between the meanings tied to people in these schools and the types of educational programs, practices and knowledge associated with different groups has been treated conceptually and empirically. Finally, the last body of educational research that we integrate is the literature that interrogates the construction and deployment of categories of student populations, particularly the "urban" or "inner city" student. This literature connects this overview back to the meanings of city spaces and people, locating the discussion in city schools in particular, as well as provides us with a conceptual mooring to the social construction of student populations.

The Apartheid Condition of City Space in the US

The dictum 'Tell me where you live and I can probably guess the type of education that you've experienced' seems to be an overarching theme in the educational literature focusing on curriculum differentiation. This literature has reported that a great deal of variability can be found in the educational experiences of residents who live in different parts of metropolitan areas. Reading across this body, there is something significant about residing in the suburbs, the city center or, even, within particular city neighborhoods that translates into encountering particular educational resources, curricula, pedagogies, or peer groups. While a great deal of the educational research frames this as a school or institutional problem, others have broadened their analysis and have argued that such differentiation is entangled with the demographic and housing patterns of these spaces (Kantor & Brenzel, 1993), as well as federal, state and regional political processes (Lipman, 2002; Orfield, 2001).

The significance of social space in shaping the processes of educational differentiation becomes evident as we come to understand the apartheid-like divisions of most cities. New York, Chicago, and Boston, among other cities, have historically been ethnically and racially divided cities. Each has its own version of a South Side or West End that has been home to immigrants and the city's resident black population. Each also has a wealthy and white Gold Coast or Manhattan. The inner city of Boston, for example, had its North and West End that had been the home to various groups of newly arrived immigrants. These crowded housing areas, comprised of multi-family tenements, provided many immigrants with a multi-ethnic space that was spatially and culturally distinct from earlier generations of immigrants and established white residents (Ward, 1989).

For southern black migrants arriving in New York City during the 1916 Great Migration, discriminatory housing patterns contributed greatly to the establishment of the predominately black inner-city neighborhood of Harlem. White property owners relegated blacks to a bounded and distinct space contained by the Harlem River, Amsterdam Avenue and Central Park. These neighborhoods became a racially homogenous space as whites fled to other parts of the city. A similar pattern would emerge in Chicago's South Side, as well as in Central Philadelphia (Meyer, 2000). Dual worlds were forged in these cities with semi-separate economies, cultural centers and spheres of community (Drake & Clayton, 1970). Housing segregation allowed black entrepreneurs, professionals and artists to flourish amid the captive clientele. Stephan Meyer (2000) notes, "Whites accepted Harlem as a black enclave, and as long as African Americans stayed within Harlem's borders, race relations remained tranquil" (p. 32).

This pattern of racially distinct city spaces has not diminished over time. In fact, many have documented how city spaces have become more and more racially divided over the last fifty years (Jackson, 1985; Meyer, 2000; Wilson, 1987). Douglas Massey and Nancy Denton (1993) have described how African-Americans have experienced "hypersegregation" (p. 74), or segregation along multiple planes of isolation or centralization, over the last fifty years as inner cities have become inhabited predominately by African-Americans and new generations of immigrants. After cities experienced a degree of social integration due to the concentration of factory work at the turn of the 20th century (Jackson, 1985; Ward, 1989), the pattern of racial segregation intensified as suburbs were built outside of metropolitan areas. They note that as the white, middle class took flight to suburbs outside of cities, African-Americans as well as a few other ethnic minority groups (e.g., Mexicans, Chinese) found themselves locked in segregated city spaces (see also Jackson, 1985). Unable to secure loans to buy homes or break through discriminatory restrictive covenants in suburbs, these groups were left in a state of social and economic isolation.

With this isolation, the landscape of inner cities also experienced an economic change in the terrain. The few industrial and manufacturing jobs that survived the post-industrial turn that began in the early 1970s also fled city centers and were relocated in the suburbs (Castells, 2000; Jackson, 1985; Kantor & Brenzal, 1993; Wilson, 1987). This movement took with it jobs and taxes that kept many inner-city neighborhoods economically viable. For example, Jean Anyon (1997) reports that Camden and Newark (New Jersey) suffered massive unemployment as New Jersey lost over 81,000 manufacturing jobs during the 1980s. Alongside this trend towards deindustrialization, suburban oriented legislatures and voters enacted fiscally conservative tax policies that redistributed tax income to favor suburbs. As the tax base dropped, many of the city services that kept inner-city spaces functioning were minimized or disappeared altogether. A black working class was created without work (Wilson, 1987). For the poor who were not employed prior to this economic turn, the landscape only became more dire as storefronts dwindled. In some cities, such as Milwaukee (Wisconsin),

Detroit (Michigan) and certain parts of inner-city Chicago (Illinois), the departure of businesses and the white middle class choked particular parts of these cities to the point that only vacant buildings, dilapidated housing projects and the non-working poor remained (Anyon, 1997; Jones, Newman & Isay, 1997; Wilson, 1987).

Most recently, the hypersegregation that Massey and Denton (1993) documented has manifested into a fragmented, or segmented, central city space within some urban areas, rather than a strictly white suburb and black central city divide (also see Castells, 2000, Haymes, 1995 and Noguera, 2003). This fragmentation is characterized by the segmentation of different areas of city spaces along the lines of different racial and social classed groups that claim and are relegated to particular segments of the city. While business centers have long been one such segment, gentrification efforts undertaken during the 1980s and 1990s in many cities have displaced low socio-economic immigrant and black communities from particular neighborhoods. These city initiated activities have created white, middle-class neighborhoods under the auspices of "revitalizing" and "preserving" the city (Boyer, 1986; Castells, 2000; Haymes, 1995). The result of these changes in some cities is a patchwork of different neighborhoods, varying in their populations, services and appearance (Noguera, 2003). Christine Boyer (1990) describes this fragmented space in noting that cities have become

> hierarchicalized into high/low ensembles—luxury areas, middle-class residential neighborhoods, historical centers, profitable areas—which are juxtaposed against the abandoned areas of the city, its slums, immigrant districts and poorer sections. (p. 102)

This fragmentation does not negate that city and suburban spaces are racially and economically segregated. The suburbs have remained generally white and middle class. Processes of gentrification have added a layer of complexity to understanding some city spaces (e.g., Los Angeles, New York, Chicago) as having intramural divisions.

These transformations of city spaces do not happen overnight, nor are there solely negative consequences to some of these shifts in some cities. Populations of new immigrants from abroad and black migrants from the South slowly replaced white residents who sought "safer" (i.e., white) neighborhoods and open space (Jackson, 1985; Sanjek, 1998; Ward, 1989). The new populations that moved into city centers remade them by replacing existing white oriented businesses and churches with new ones that catered to the sensibilities and tastes of the new residents. Roger Sanjek (1998) documented such a transformation in chronicling the in-flow of Puerto Rican, Korean, and Haitian families into the Elmhurst-Corona section of New York City as whites fled farther to the outer suburbs of New York City. As these groups settled in this community, they moved from renting apartments in the Elmhurst-Corona neighborhood to, ultimately, purchasing houses that were once owned by white residents, despite encountering a great deal of discriminatory lending practices.

Furthermore, the demographic and geographic shifts of the Elmhurst-Corona area brought out the cultural richness of each different community as the built environment was altered to reflect the change in population. In this case, the "new multicultural geography" (Sanjek, 1998) gave rise to a social integration that this part of the city had never experienced. New rituals and artistic traditions intermixed as a plurality of different ethnic and racial groups cohabitated within the same space. Sanjek (1998) explains the fluidity of this co-mingling:

> [C]ultural juxtaposition characterized Elmhurst-Corona, and peoples and languages ran into each other in a mix never seen before. Their businesses, whether ethnically distinctive or not, were interspersed, and many depended on a mixed clientele. On a heavily Latin American block of Roosevelt Avenue in Elmhurst, an Indian, a Chinese, and a Korean store coexisted with seven Colombian, Dominican, and Argentinean firms; and facing William Moore Park in Corona, one Jewish, one Korean, two Greek, and two Dominican stores were scattered among fourteen Italian businesses. (p. 223)

The integration found in the Elmhurst-Corona district reflects the resilient side of various communities in light of economic and demographic shifts. Sanjek recognizes that community members engaged in a great deal of political contestation, work, and coalition building to keep this part of the city a thriving neighborhood. He acknowledges, though, that the minimal presence of African-Americans within the area raises questions about the degree of integration in this part of the city.

While some central cities, such as Elmhurst-Corona, survived, and some might say surmounted, surburbanization trends, the point that politicians, white elites and corporations engineered racially distinct sections of cities–racially diverse Elmhurst-Corona and white, upper-class Manhattan, in Sanjek's case–cannot not be lost. The social, political and economic capital that is lost when inner cities become primarily immigrant and black enclaves has significant consequences on the lives of people. That is, as the white middle class flees so does the attention of politicians, as well as the social and economic power base (Jacobs, 1998; Wilson, 1996). Furthermore, as city spaces become less integrated, and contact between different ethnic and racial groups decreases, particular assumptions thrive about city spaces and the people that reside there.

The Production of Meanings of City Spaces

As discriminatory housing practices and settlement patterns rendered city spaces racially distinct, city residents have tied particular racialized meanings and assumptions to these spaces and their inhabitants. Specifically, designations of a morally and orderly white population and space were juxtaposed to ethnic and racial groups and their space that were supposedly immoral, dirty and chaotic (Haymes, 1995; Jackson, 1985; Ward, 1989). Inner cities and their inhabitants have historically been inscribed with the latter characteristics, whereas white suburbs were typically employed to describe the former. Newspapers and magazines have historically functioned to imprint in the imaginations of metropolitan area residents an image of immigrant spaces as slums at the turn of 20th century. The term "slum" acquired a meaning that defined these spaces as bastions of depravity and absolute poverty (Ward, 1989). Its residents, meanwhile, were defined as morally depraved and inclined towards pauperism and criminality. These meanings were stated unabashedly, for example, in the images and language of popular culture at the time as representations of the Irish, or 'Paddy,' depicted an irresponsible delinquency (Takaki, 1994; Ward, 1989).

Scientific work was not immune from participating in the production of these meanings either. Social scientists produced a "symbolic language for the politics of race" (Edsall & Edsall, 1992; Jacobs, 1998) as they masked race and racist presuppositions in scientific discourse. The same propositions of the immoral and the enlightened were articulated in academic research as social workers and social geographers employed ecological frameworks to map the social realm of cities using frameworks that denoted particular parts of cities as "zones of blight and delinquency," and, contrastedly, "zones of assimilation" (Ward, 1989). The work of University of Chicago sociologists Robert Park (1925) and Clifford Shaw and Henry MacKay (1931) typified this line of research. Their work established hierarchies between these different city spaces. They also introduced a language of pathologies that they overlaid upon the black and immigrant residents who lived in what they scientifically deemed "zones of blight." The overlap between the zones of blight and delinquency with the spaces inhabited by black and immigrant populations in the inner cities surely had a powerful effect in solidifying the images that circulated in popular culture. A discourse of the culture of poverty and the deficit arose to the stature of science (Menchaca, 1997).

As the term "slum" gave way to the use of the racialized construct of "the ghetto" after World War I, the historical connotations of particular areas and people remained stable throughout the suburbanization movement that took place between 1940 and 1980. For the white middle class, the inner city, particularly black neighborhoods, has consistently been a place of danger and delinquency. Yet, various authors have argued that alongside the image of immorality and crime, the inner city has also been underpinned as a space of pleasure and desire for the white elite and middle class. Stephen Haymes (1995) argues that for whites the "black ghetto" represented an adult playground where they could unleash their sexual freedom. They saw these spaces as locales where they could engage in exotic activities with "exotic" people. This imagery was predicated on racialized social meanings that conceptualized blacks as hypersexual and primitive. Symbolically, whites termed such inner-city spaces, specifically black communities, as "jungles" of immorality. Black communities did not share this outlook, however. Many African-Americans viewed, instead, their neighborhoods as "homeplaces" (hooks, 1990; Haymes, 1995) that were "erected in their own image" (Drake and Clayton, 1970, p. 115). The power that lied in the mainstream machinery of communication (e.g., newspapers, novels, popular culture) propagated the dominant message that these were dangerous and immoral spaces and people, however.

White, suburban spaces and people were also entangled within this symbolic language of the politics of race, though not in the same way as black communities. While the dark and blighted inner city represented danger and moral release, the white and green-lawned suburban spaces were explicitly juxtaposed as safe, orderly, and rational (Haymes, 1995; Jackson, 1985). The suburb was sold to the white middle class and white ethnics as a place of security and pastoral existence (Jackson, 1985; Jacobs, 1998; Ward, 1998). Developers and marketers coupled physical health and longevity to suburban life. For example, an 1871 advertisement for a Louisville suburb stated, "[South park] is just the place for dozens of families of the city with tendency to consumption, since a home in this pine forest would prolong their life many years" (cited in Jackson, 1985, pp. 69-70). The industrialist Henry Ford surmised in more apocalyptic terms, "The city is doomed," and "We shall solve the city problem by leaving the city" (cited in Jackson, 1985, p. 175).

By the mid- to latter part of the 20th century, the suburbs came to symbolize what Kenneth Jackson (1985) documents as "relief from the pervasive fear of racial integration and its two presumed fellow travelers—interracial violence and interracial sex" (p. 290). The mode of talking about city and suburban spaces and their inhabitants, as well as the manner of expressing white fear and resentment, though, took on a public tone of race neutrality as black communities challenged physically (i.e., race riots of Detroit and Watts) and legally (i.e., *Brown vs. Topeka* and the litigation that followed) overt racist practices (Jacobs, 1998). While the new terms of talking about race and city-suburban space never stated race explicitly, white politicians and white owned newspapers deployed a specific vocabulary that continued to name race through coded language that had clear meanings to white populations. In other words, white politicians and the media propelled new instantiations of the symbolic language of the politics of race that were earlier the domain of social scientists (Edsall & Edsall, 1992; Jacobs, 1998). This language included codes such as "urban," "busing," and "desegregation" (Jacobs, 1998). These constructs were filled with racial overtones by white residents, politicians, business leaders and the media.

A case in point is the city of Columbus, Ohio. Gregory Jacobs (1998) describes how white real estate agents, developers and bankers sold the suburbs of Columbus to white buyers in the 1970s with advertisements such as "Don't bus, come live with us" (p. 133), and "DeSegregation means DeUrbanization" (p. 133). As the Columbus City School Board began to discuss the possibility of integrating schools through busing, real estate agents and developers seized upon this language and redeployed it in a way to convey to whites an imagery of safety, tranquility and, ultimately, distance from the inner-city "jungle." The effects of this use of language in media advertisement and the machinery of development (i.e., banking and developers) were the flight of whites from the city as well as a consolidated move by banks, real estate agents and developers to divest their resources from the city limits of Columbus. A divided city was produced, one area inhabited by middle- and upper-class whites and the other by working class blacks.

These meanings were still a pervasive part of popular culture in the 1980s and 1990s as popular movies re-inscribed meanings of the city and the suburbs. Films such as *Grand Canyon, Menace II Society, Falling Down* and *Boyz 'N the Hood* all propped up the imagery of the dangerous and dark (i.e., black) inner city and the safe and orderly (i.e., white) suburb (McCarthy, Rodriguez, Buendía, Meacham, David, Wilson-Brown, Godina, 1997). The image of the black, male thug accosting the white, family oriented suburbanite in a post-industrial city backdrop was a central narrative in most of these films. The cultural meanings that circulated in these texts defined security as a physical distancing of oneself from black and non-white ethnics, and sheltering oneself in white enclaves.

The symbolic language of the politics of race within cities has retained the façade of race neutrality in the last 20 years. Within many cities, this language has sought to convey meanings of desirability that have sought to draw in investors from around the world. City politicians and the media have been central to these processes of meaning making. City politicians in New York City and Chicago participated in deeming particular areas of their respective cities as more favorable than others by affiliating them with economic activities. Roger Sanjek (1998) notes that Mayor Edward Koch's designation of New York City as "Headquarter City" and, later, "World City" ideologically foregrounded the city's financial institutions and leisure amenities for the elite, monied class, at the expense of the city's immigrant and working class. Pauline Lipman (2002) makes a similar case in examining Mayor Richard Daley's designation and marketing of Chicago as a "Global City." She found that city schools were tailored to attract the white, middle and upper classes. Both authors argue that such designations align city policies and practices to particular priorities and constituents. The beneficiaries of these policies and practices are, many times, the corporate sector and those white, middle- and elite-class spaces (i.e., neighborhoods) and residents of the city that have already been discursively constructed as the most deserving and capable of capitalizing on the benefits from such activities.

Differentiated School Spaces

While metropolitan spaces have been divided in an apartheid-like manner, public education institutions in most metropolitan areas have been equally segregated by race and social class. The educational literature is replete with analyses that show that metropolitan schools mirror the racial and class divisions found in city landscapes (Kantor & Brenzel, 1996; Kozol, 1992; Noguera, 2003). More specifically, the central argument provided by this literature is that not only do schools mirror these divisions, but that they are driven by the divisions in the housing and economic realms. In the period following the Brown decision (post-1954), a resilient pattern emerged where the majority of the students in central city schools are children of color who are poor, and those in suburban schools are predominately white and middle class. For example, Gary Orfield (1984) studied cities such as Chicago and Detroit and identified a pattern where the majority of students in inner city schools were African-American. In 1980, 60 percent of the students in Chicago's public schools were African-American and close to 20 percent were Latino (Orfield, 1984). In all, close to 60 percent of the central city school population was from low-income families. Chicago's suburban schools, on the other hand, were predominately white, or 85 percent. Only 9 percent of the suburban school student body were from low-income families. The same pattern held for Detroit. Orfield (1996) concludes, "By 1990, metropolitan Detroit had the most intense residential segregation in the United States and its black students were more segregated than any other metropolitan area except Chicago" (p. 315).

Harvey Kantor and Barbara Brenzel's (1993) analysis of residential and school segregation literature reports similar findings in other metropolitan areas such as Milwaukee and Los Angeles. Where African Americans generally comprised the most isolated population in central city schools, Latinos in Los Angeles became the largest group to experience the effects of school isolation during the 1980s. Kantor and Brenzel, alongside Orfield (1996), note that only within the South, where the courts pressed heavily for desegregation policy, were patterns of racial segregation interrupted.

Differentiated School Knowledge

With school populations mirroring the racial and class divide that exists in city schools, researchers have found that differences also exist in the curricular programs and knowledge found in these different educational spaces. Generally, studies have identified a pattern where a "low status" content knowledge, or knowledge having little exchange value (i.e., social and economic) in US culture and higher education settings (Oakes, 1985), is taught to students of color (i.e., African-Americans, Latinos, Native

Americans) who are poor. "High status" knowledge and course offerings, on the other hand, are more readily available to middle-class whites. The great majority of these analyses have focused on academic tracking in high schools. The well cited work of Jeannie Oakes (1985) on the link between race and class and academic tracking exemplifies how access to content knowledge in US high schools is hinged on race and class affiliation. She notes:

> While there is certainly no automatic placement of poor and minority students in low tracks or of affluent white students in upper tracks, the odds of being assigned into particular tracks are not equal. In virtually every study that has considered this question, poor and minority students have been found in disproportionately large percentages in the bottom groups. (Oakes, 1985, p. 64)

This pattern has been corroborated and expanded upon analytically by other researchers who have observed that the distribution of high status and low status knowledge in US high schools breaks up into an inner-city and suburb split (Kantor & Brenzel, 1993; Oakes, 1985). The fact that inner cities are composed of children of color and the suburbs are white and middle class has led to different achievement rates in these different areas (Kantor & Brenzel, 1993; Orfield, 1996). Less than half of the ninth graders who enter high schools in large cities graduate in the traditional four year period (Anyon, 1997; Haney, 2000). Results of the National Assessment of Education Progress show that while reading and math scores rose for African Americans and Latinos in the 1970s and 1980s, the scores for these populations attending inner-city schools were significantly lower than those nationally (Kantor & Brenzel, 1993).

The way that city schools structure these varied outcomes has been described in various studies, the majority generally conceptualizing the school as a somewhat internal (i.e., isolated) unit. The dimensions that have been named include a fragmented and teacher centered, or defensive, mode of teaching that stifles any real student learning (McNeil, 2000), to a subtractive educational ethic practiced by teachers in high schools that have linguistically diverse populations (Valenzuela, 1996). Other analyses have broadened their analytical plane and have identified more systemic sets of relationships such as the "dumbing-down" of curriculum as forces of accountability and high stakes testing pressure schools to produce results (Lipman, 2002; McNeil, 2000) to the disparities in the funding practices of particular states (Kozol, 1994).

One argument that has been proffered to explain the disparity between different groups is that within educational tracks and particular schools as a whole, teachers practice a defensive pedagogy. Linda McNeil (1999) defines this method of instruction as one where content is "tightly controlled by teachers, reduced to simplistic fragments, and treated with little regard for a reference to resources in the students' experiences or school's references" (p. 159). Within this type of instruction, students are provided with a knowledge that is reduced to trivia, and one that can be condensed to a lecture or a worksheet. What is missing in this approach are opportunities for students to acquire processing skills of knowledge production and integration of knowledge with their own personal experiential base.

A similar explanation has been offered in discussing Latino drop out. Angela Valenzuela's (1996) examination of the reasons and processes that prompt Mexican and Mexican American/Chicano students to disinvest in learning and school points to an institutional ethic, which she terms "aesthetic caring." She, like McNeil and others (Fine, 1991), identifies how high school teachers pedagogically and socially engage students in an administrative, institutional fashion. In this mode, she argues, administrators and teachers teach and interact with students in ways that strip them of the cultural capital (i.e., linguistic, cultural and social resources) that they bring to the school setting. That is, schooling becomes a subtractive process rather than an additive one. The mode of teaching and the organization of the curriculum deem the linguistic and knowledge assets that students bring to school contexts as having little value. The effect of such practices is that students are placed on the margins of the curriculum and school life (Gitlin, Buendía, Crossland, & Doumbia, 2003; Valdés, 2001).

While teachers bear the brunt of the blame in these studies, the recent writings of these and other authors (Gitlin, Buendía, Crosland & Doumbia, 2003; Haney, 2000; McNeil, 2000; Valenzuela, 2002) expand the analytical field to recognize that these approaches to teaching are entangled with other bureaucratic mechanisms that connect school processes to broader social relations other than teachers' personal attitudes or beliefs. Various researchers have identified how federal and state mandated standardization and accountability initiatives function as powerful forces (Lipman, 2002; McNeil & Valenzuela, 1998). The unifying theme emerging from this literature is that federal and state mandated testing, which have high stake consequences on students' retention and high school graduation, have reduced teaching within inner-city schools to a pedagogy of drills and test preparation. Valenzuela (2003) points to the Houston Independent School District (HISD) as an example of this trend. The state of Texas and the HISD reformed its retention, promotion and graduation standards such that students had to pass exit exams, such as the Texas Assessment of Academic Skills (TASS) for graduation, to advance from one grade to the next. When students failed the exam, HISD assigned these high school students to remedial courses entitled "TAAS-Math" and "TAAS-Reading," courses aimed at preparing students for the exit tests. Students took these courses in place of the regular curriculum, yet did not receive high school credit. Even high performing magnet schools within states such as Texas have been transformed to a curriculum of "packaged fragments of information" (McNeil, 2000, p. 3).

The concentration of these particular types of compensatory curricula and pedagogy within inner cities is an important point in this work, even though the geographical dimension has been generally subsumed or unexplored in this body of work. As segregation within inner cities intensifies, the higher the likelihood that these defensive and compensatory curricula and teaching strategies will be in found in these places (Orfield, 1996; Valenzuela, 2003). To put this differently, it seems that a specific spatial clustering of educational programs and curricula are found as particular racial populations of children are geographically concentrated, breaking down, many times, along the lines of suburban and inner-city designations.

One of the few studies to link the city's geography and curriculum offerings was conducted by Pauline Lipman (2002). She found that Chicago's Public School's policies on program placement reproduced historical patterns of city segregation. Examining the city as a whole, she mapped the geographical placement of new high school programs and found a pattern in which the majority of the academic, college preparatory programs, what she termed "plus" programs (i.e., Magnet high schools, International Baccalaureate, Math and Science Academies), were geographically located within parts of the city that were inhabited by white and affluent residents—residential areas having a long history of white, upper middle-class residents as well as areas of the city that were undergoing gentrification. The "minus" programs, or those that were compensatory in their focus (i.e., Vocational Education, Direct Instruction), were concentrated, for the most, in poor communities with high numbers of Latinos and African-Americans. The terms the city deployed for this distribution of programs were making Chicago a competitive global city and providing equality to all.

Methodologically, Lipman's examination offers researchers and educators a way to understand the implications of city's governmental decisions on producing differentiated schooling. She holds that city schools are victims of the politics of cities, especially as schools are forced to comply with new accountability mechanisms. Furthermore, her study helps us to conceptualize city spaces as segmented at the level of schools, as pockets of different educational communities who experience different educational programs. The divisions she explores do not follow a traditional suburban/inner-city split. She shows that what transpires programmatically in some large city school districts varies from neighborhood to neighborhood, contingent upon the historically recurrent variables of race and social class. Lastly, the study also facilitates an understanding of how student identities are constituted as a result of the spatial coordination of curricula. She interjects a spatial element to the processes of social reproduction that nods to the opening point that framed this chapter regarding the relationship between neighborhood and the type of educational program.

Taken as a whole, all of the educational literature that we have discussed thus far to situate our examination suggests that differentiated educational experiences are an effect of structural relations. Study after study reports how schools make differentiations as a result of segregated populations that emerge from housing segregation, the outcomes of standardized tests, or the tradition of educational tracking. While this explanation is compelling in its argumentation and evidence, it needs to be broadened in order to attend to the complexity of schools and broader contexts that are not solely bound to the structural domain. Prior to the systemic implementation of these exams within many states, schools and teachers were engaged in processes of differentiation around vocational and classical liberal educational programs (Kantor, 1988; Kliebard, 1986; Tyack & Cuban, 1995), and the education of black and white children (Anderson, 1988). Some suggest that there is an element of power in the cultural meanings themselves of what it means to be an "inner-city" population and, implicitly, an "urban" student. A small body of literature has begun to explore this dimension and argue that such constructs are equally as powerful as structural relations in shaping the definition of needs, programs and knowledge allocation. This literature has begun to explore the relationships between the meanings of the ecology (objects and people) of the inner city that Haymes and Ward identified and the discourses of difference that have been constructed in city schools in making differentiations in curriculum and pedagogy.

Institutional Construction of Student Identity

The line of research focusing on the cultural meanings of the inner-city or urban student has begun to explore how the politics of knowledge work to construct particular populations. The analytical turn of this research is towards the knowledge that comes to bear to construct individuals and populations within institutional settings. Institutional group identity in this body of work is conceptualized as discursive, or as a system of language, and historically constructed rather than viewed as a biological essence. Similar to the discussions of the meanings of city spaces, this small body of educational literature has focused its attention to examining the institutional meanings that are attached to particular groups of people to construct difference in student populations.

Such analyses have been conducted by various researchers (Lee, 1996; McKay & Wong, 1996; Popkewitz, 1998B) on the constructs of the "model minority," "E.S.L," "inner city" and "urban" student. Thomas Popkewitz's (1998B) study of the knowledge that is brought to bear in inner-city schools shows how different discourses are overlaid, or what he terms scaffolding, to create a subject constituted as the inner-city student. Central to his work is the premise that particular attributes of difference are ascribed to "make" the urban and rural student and, ultimately, space. He states:

> This approach to research suggests that there is no child, as an object of study, in a school until discursive strategies are applied to enable one to "see," think, talk, and feel about the object of study in school. In this sense, the urbanness and ruralness of the school and the child is "made" through the scaffolding of discourses about the child, teaching, and learning. Thus, to approach the assumptions about urban and rural schools, research cannot regard them as geographical concepts; they are discursive concepts that historically circulate in schooling to construct the qualities and capabilities of the urban and rural child. (p. 9)

Popkewitz's emphasis on the term "made" argues that the institutional construct of the rural and urban child is an assemblage of historical discourses stemming from 19th century views of education as rescue, state welfare policies from the 1960s and current theories of child development that come from psychology. These constructs of the urban and suburban exist within a binary in which the latter sits unstated. Through these discourses, he argues, a space of the urban and suburban are constructed. Alongside the urban/suburban binary, other important binaries of difference are implied (i.e., black/white, smart/dumb, norm/deviant) that insert discursive distinctions between students identified as urban and suburban populations, as well as between space.

Where Popkewitz (1998B) foregrounds social and behavioral science discourses in the construction of students, others exploring the productive elements of these distinctions have found other discourses besides those found in science. Angela Valenzuela (1999), Patrick Solomon (1992) and Cameron McCarthy (1998) show how students and educators deploy discourses from popular culture within educational institutions to mark out racial and ethnic difference. As an example, the meanings of popular culture and media discourses become central in Valenzuela's (1999) explanation of why high school teachers read Mexican-American students as "not caring" about school and, conversely, Mexican immigrants as "caring." Valenzuela notes that as students deploy the clothing, hair styles and music found in popular culture, teachers decode these signs as gestures of anti-education. The same argument is found in Solomon's (1992) study of Jamaican high school students within Canadian schools. Valenzuela, too, identifies a mode of binary logic that Popkewitz identifies. Where Mexican Americans/Chicanos are viewed as uninterested and lazy, Mexican immigrants, who are often clean cut and inclined to wear conservative attire, are discursively interpreted as pro-education. These constructions, Valenzuela holds, are part of the machinery that are work in institutionally creating programmatic distinctions among students. While she does not conceptually frame these constructions as systems of ideas, as Popkewitz does, their theses intersect conceptually on the idea that a project of construction is at work, and that it comes to play in the designation and differentiation of programs and the treatment from educators.

Hence, cultural meanings, drawing from this literature, become important elements in understanding how particular orderings and rationalizations are imposed in the organization of material relations. It opens up, analytically, the realm of cultural constructs as a focal point for understanding how particular subjects are constituted, and how these socially constructed subjects are enmeshed with the structural ecology of environments.

The Landscape of Our Examination

These three bodies of literature–the production of city spaces, the distribution of school knowledge and programs, and the construction of the inner-city student–form the landscape in which we situate our study of the production of the West Side, East Side and Central City school and student. Our ensuing analysis and discussion will intersect these bodies of literature as a means of showing and theorizing how the social organization of city space, and the city-wide meanings of these spaces work in concert with schools, as schools participate in the production of the West Side, East Side and Central City school and student. These bodies will facilitate the connection of contextual relations in ways that will help readers to see how current patterns of re-segregation of people and school knowledge go hand-in-hand with the social construction of these spaces and the people who inhabit them.

CHAPTER 2

KNOWLEDGE, THE PRACTICE OF DIFFERENCE, AND SOCIAL SPACE

The goal of this project is to understand the relationship between the fragmented organization and meanings of city spaces and the differentiation of students, at the level of student ontology and school curricular practices, which occurs in elementary schools that lie in different parts of cities. To accomplish this, we need conceptual tools that will allow us to understand the interplay between the ecological context of cities and the school processes that construct these differences. To put this a little differently, we need analytical units that permit us to move beyond the walls of schools and the heads of educators to account for shared meanings that are institutionalized across city and school spaces.

In this chapter, we develop a conceptual framework that centers on the units knowledge, practices of difference, technologies and social space. We devote a great deal of attention to defining these constructs by locating them within the various theoretical literatures, as well as specifying why they are of importance in educational research focusing on processes of differentiating students and curricula in urban schools. Specifically, this chapter draws from overlapping bodies of social theory and critical educational research, with particular emphasis on the theorizing of Michel Foucault, Henri Lefebvre, and Edward Soja. We tie elements of their respective theories together so that their relationship is seen as constitutive. This relationship becomes what we frame as a trialectic, a concept we borrow from Soja (1996). Trialectical reasoning is an integrative mechanism and process that is able to attend to multiple dimensions without ever needing to reconcile tensions. Soja (1996) describes the trialectic as "a mode of dialectical reasoning that is more inherently spatial than the temporally defined dialectic of Marx and Hegel" (p. 10, 1996). It is a construct that is inclined to the "radical openness" of a third variable, possibility, or outcome (Soja, p. 56, 1996). It will be a concept that will help us to discuss overlapping fields and social relations that comprise urban spaces that resist binary modes of thinking and that exist without being integrated into preexisting continuities.

Knowledge

In Chapter 1, we identified how particular meanings of city spaces have been historically created by city residents, the media and academicians. An argument that paralleled the construction of city spaces was offered in the literature around the construction of subjects institutionally called the "urban" student. The tool that we will employ to analyze for these meanings is that of knowledge. The concept of knowledge is one that has had different definitions over time, however. Competing conceptions can be found in circulation in the philosophical doctrines dating back to Plato and Aristotle (Toulmin, 1972; White, 1982). Rather than attempt to discuss all of the different frameworks of knowledge, we focus our attention on the epistemological and axiological tenets of knowledge construction and validation as they have been defined in modernist and what some have termed post-structuralist philosophical frameworks. It is with the latter framing of knowledge, as discourses institutionalized as truths, with which we will ultimately align ourselves in order to analyze the knowledge of the East Side, West Side and Central City student, school and space.

The concept of knowledge as neutral, objectivist truth has been anchored in Western society by an Enlightenment mode of reasoning and a machinery of social relations that we have come to identify as the markers of modernity. The philosophies and axioms of Hugo Grotius, René Descartes, and Isaac Newton ushered in a faith in rules and procedures of reason that have undergirded knowledge and its 'discovery' as of the 17th century (Toulmin, 1992). These rules and procedures were formulated as vehicles to discern and adjudicate truth over myth and reasoned thought over emotional impulse. Central to this line of thought was the assertion of dichotomies that separated the realms of nature and humanity, the mind and the body, as well as the physical world from the spiritual one. The premise of this dichotomous line of reasoning was that on one side lay the orderly, and on the other the disorderly. By establishing such dichotomies, proponents of the Enlightenment mode of reasoning proffered that it brought purity to knowledge by stripping away the subjective clouds of bodily (or that of the carnal and emotional) and godly (or the political) intervention.

The purity of knowledge was established through the rationalist and, ultimately, objectivist standpoint of knowledge. While many have discussed this worldview at length (Delanty, 2000; Denzin 1997; Toulmin 1992), let us briefly outline some of the central elements. As Descartes and others demarcated the lines of the orderly and the disorderly, as well as the reasoned and unreasoned, humanity was positioned as inclined towards orderly thought. Stephen Toulmin (1992) identifies how philosophers established this relationship through axioms that expanded upon the humanity dimension of the nature/humanity dichotomy. One of the central axioms of the rationalist project was:

> *The essence of Humanity is the capacity for rational thought and action.* Following Descartes, Newton took "experience" to mean the totality of sensory inputs that enter the Inner Theatre of the conscious mind, and the logical operations performed upon them during rational deliberation. All this occurs (Descartes implies) in an "unextended" realm of thought, locally associated with–but not causally dependent on–physiological mechanisms in the brain. (p. 113)

This tenet conceptually positioned humanity with the ability to capture the orderly unfoldings of nature. The mind/brain link positioned humans with the ability to engage in "rational thought and action" that was detached from the body. Ultimately, and most importantly, the conscious mind was attributed as capable of identifying the natural rules of reason that made rational, objective deliberation and knowledge possible.

The rules of reason were further delineated and carried forward in the early to mid-20th century with the articulation of Logical Positivism. The writings of Bertrand Russell and Rudolph Carnup, among others, coupled procedures of knowledge production–such as observation, measurement, and validation–to mathematical operations, specifically the interpretation of 'sensory data' using inductive logic. The argument underpinning this move was a belief that the realm of the natural and the social had to be equally as orderly and perfect as the principles and propositions constituting mathematical reasoning. Furthermore, philosophers and, ultimately, theorists banked on a realist premise of ontology that held that accessing and understanding nature was an unmediated and unfettered process (Denzin, 1997). Hence, the orthodoxy of the time was that if the researcher could visibly see the phenomenon, "he" could design a way to capture its essence by quantitatively measuring it to explain its operation. Once it was captured, the propositions of truth would emerge from nature to form a body of knowledge.

The preparation of generations of researchers with these rules and procedures solidified this view of knowledge and knowledge discovery over the last two centuries (Kuhn, 1970). With the rules and procedures of validation in hand, scientists were licensed to objectively discover the natural systems and laws of the material world (Rosaldo, 1989). The focus on procedures and rules of validation left the question of the properties of knowledge and its production as a foregone conclusion. Thomas Kuhn (1970) expanded on this point by arguing that these scientists were trained to ask questions and validate results within received paradigms, or what he refers to as "models of scientific practice from which spring particular coherent traditions of scientific research" (p. 10). These modes of posing questions and procedures of validation ensured, to some extent, the longevity of a particular type of science and scientific rationality. Kuhn (1970) states:

> The study of paradigms...is what mainly prepares the student for membership in the particular scientific community with which he [sic] will later practice. Because he [sic] there joins men [sic] who learned the bases of their field from the same concrete models, his [sic] subsequent practice will seldom evoke overt disagreement over fundamentals. Men whose research is based on shared paradigms are committed to the same rules and standards for scientific practice. That commitment and the apparent consensus it produces are prerequisites for normal science, i.e., for the genesis and continuation of a particular research tradition. (pp. 10-11)

The establishment and dissemination of rules and procedures of experimentation and validation are important in the foundation of disciplines and disciplinary knowledge. Scientists' ability to know is enmeshed in these systems of rationality. Where Descartes and, later, most Logical Positivists (e.g., Rudolf Carnup, Carl Hempel, Karl Popper) considered group membership an insignificant factor to knowledge production, Kuhn emphasized the relevance of these relationships by arguing that the inculcation of particular ways of acting and knowing are key factors in forming what is deemed "normal" or accepted science. It has been argued that Kuhn's analysis of knowledge production and paradigmatic changes in the natural sciences ushered in a view of knowledge and its production that departed radically from the modernist view that framed scientists as detached and objective in asking their questions.

Revisions to the Received View of Knowledge

Where the Enlightenment view of knowledge and truth emphasized the imposition of rules of reasoned logic, a realist ontological standpoint and the incremental growth of knowledge, others, besides Kuhn, have departed from rule driven theories of knowledge discovery and have identified other mechanisms and processes at work to define knowledge. The modernist view has been confronted by competing theories of knowledge that have challenged the neutral, objectivist, discovery oriented worldview. Many of these other frameworks, often termed postmodernist, have entered the conversation with a sense of attempting to understand the production, or social construction, of truth(s) and its relationship to the varying concepts of humanity and nature that have emerged historically. Where modernist frameworks have emphasized objective discovery, a central premise of many of these other frameworks is that knowledge is relational and socially produced. Discussions of the power of ideology and, more recently, of discourse have prompted social theorists to rethink knowledge frameworks. Tom Popkewitz (1998A) articulates this shift in noting, "How people tell the truth about the world is part of and expressive of social transformations by which relationships with the world and our "selves" are established" (p. 71).

Many have stated that the relationship between the seen and knowledge is socially constructed by ideology, discourses or other mediating technologies and apparatuses that rework how and what we know. Theorists such as Raymond Williams (1977) and John Berger (1972) argued long ago that our perceptions of the real are affected by learnt assumptions about our self and the real. They posited that seeing is entwined in systems of knowing (e.g., what is beauty, truth, knowledge) that are mediated through changing contexts and social technologies (e.g., photography). Contemporary theorists, specifically feminist and feminists of color such as Judith Butler (1999), Gloria Anzaldua (1987) and Patricia Hill Collins (1991), among others, have taken this thesis further to identify how systems of reasoning, or discourse, circulated in science, popular culture and literary traditions shape how "selves" are socially constructed, performed and known. They have seized upon the ideological and discursive elements to argue that the knowledge of self and her surroundings is always comprised of socially mediated ideological and discursive systems. However, prior to our discussion of how discourse operates in shaping how we see, act, and ultimately know, allow us to explain how earlier theorists, such as Karl Marx and, later, Louis Althusser, theorized the relationship between knowledge, ideology and the self. This explanation will help to contextualize, in some respects, the discussion of discourse.

An important element in Karl Marx's analysis of society was how the capitalist system was imposed and sustained upon the working class. At the heart of this discussion was the manipulation of ideology, as systems of beliefs and assumptions, by the elite to reproduce the interests and beliefs of the proletariat so that they would not revolt against the oppressive conditions of the workplace. In some sense, we might read Marx as arguing that a working class worldview, or standpoint, was in place. Marx theorized that a consciousness–or what we might read as a knowledge or, more precisely, a false knowledge–of self and societal relations was central to the maintenance of this system. This knowledge was pivotal in creating a false consciousness that was inculcated from one generation to the other through structural relations such as the family, the place of the factory, and the juridical realm. Marx held that for the working class to buck the yoke of capitalism, it needed to recognize the inherent contradictions in this system of relations. To accomplish this, a true consciousness, one informed by the truths of science, was required that allowed the working class to transcend the relations of his or her surroundings. What is important for our purposes here is the idea that knowledge could be manipulated to form a particular type of personhood (class consciousness), as well as distort one's interpretive lenses of the world. The singularity of consciousness and knowledge begins to slip. Marx ushers in within Europe a recognition of a duality of worldviews, one true and one false.

Louis Althusser (1971) developed the elements of ideology and consciousness even further by theorizing them as forces of production in itself. He recasted the concept of knowledge by discussing its relationship to societal ideologies. He expanded upon and altered Karl Marx's argument of the ideological elements of the state and its uses of ideology for the purposes of reproducing the relations of production (i.e., division of labor, the sale and purchase of labor) by theorizing the role of schools as ideological state apparatuses (ISAs). He argued that the knowledge that was taught in schools within capitalist societies is never free of ideology. He went so far as to state that knowledge (i.e., English, French, literature, sciences, arithmetic) is bound by ideology. Althusser posited that knowledge is caught up in the systems of ideas, values, and representations that emerge from the social relationships (e.g., conditions of existence) that produce a distorted knowledge.

Central to these relationships are the ISAs, such as educational and religious institutions. Althusser argued, in what was deemed by some Marxist social theorists as a very un-Marxist analysis, that ideology exists and operates separately from the realm of economic relations as a structural (material) relation. Practices are enacted and meanings are circulated within institutions that are always ideological. Notice how Althusser frames the omnipresence of ideology in institutional practices.

> [A]n ideology always exists in an apparatus, and its practice, or practices. This existence is material. ...In every case, the ideology of ideology thus recognizes, despite its imaginary distortion, that the 'ideas' of a human subject exist in his actions, or ought to exist in his actions, and if that is not the case, it lends him other ideas corresponding to the actions (however perverse that he does perform). This ideology talks of action: I shall talk of actions inserted into *practices* [emphasis original author]. And I shall point out that these practices are governed by the rituals in which these practices are inscribed, within the *material existence of an ideological apparatus,* be it only a small part of that apparatus. (Althusser, 1971, pp. 166, 168)

The premise that individuals' participation in rituals and practices are always ideological and shaped by the educational or religious ideological apparatus shifts, ever so slightly, the locus of actions away from the Marxist base structure of economic relations. Practices, as those daily routines and actions, and knowledge are conceptualized as emerging from a semi-independent array of superstructural relations that he identifies as ISAs. Economic modes of production are no longer positioned as the determining structure. Furthermore, ideology now gains, within Althusser's theorizing, the stature of a material relation.

Althusser's analysis of ideology, ISAs, and, ultimately, knowledge is important for two reasons. First, it shifts the concept of knowledge away from objectivist frameworks that envision it as independent from societal forces. Knowledge becomes, within his theorizing, something that cannot escape ideology. It is conceptualized as enmeshed with the value systems and socio-political ideas of power, a dimension that some post-structurally oriented feminists (see Butler, 1999) and feminists of color (see Collins, 1991; Delgado Bernal, 1998) have capitalized on. The objectivist stance loses its ground in this argument as power and ideology are named as always present. Where Karl Marx viewed science as the mechanism for potentially producing knowledge that was pure and non-ideological, Althusser's argument negates that possibility. Second, Althusser's theorizing argues that ideology, or what we infer here as knowledge, has a constitutive property, paralleling, in many ways, Marx's discussion of ideology and class consciousness. Althusser argued that ideology functioned to construct how individuals came to see and name themselves, their world, and their social relations. He bridged semiological and psychoanalytic theory to argue that ideology interpellated, or summoned, individuals with signs with which they came to identify themselves and, ultimately, their interests. Hence, there is no escaping ideology in Althusser's theorizing.

Knowledge as Discursive Production

Others besides Althusser have destabilized the objectivist stance of knowledge (cf. Butler, 1999; Foucault, 1978; Lyotard, 1984). These theorists and philosophers have focused their critique, however, on the theory that knowledge discovery is naturally and incrementally expanded, and that it is unified as disciplinary bodies. These theorists have emphasized the constructive dimensions of knowledge, particularly the way that knowledge is socially and discursively produced, as well as the manner in which it is coupled to an array of social machinations that function to form constructs and subjectivities. Michel Foucault's (1978, 1980) socio-historical work on the discursive formation of sexuality and madness identified the ways in which knowledge became a productive force in defining these concepts and in disciplining, or governing, social behavior to produce social difference. Central to Foucault's work is his conceptualization of knowledge as discourse, and its relationship to power. He defined discourse as durable propositions, or linguistic statements, that have a semantic coherence within particular spaces that are practiced (Foucault, 1972). But rather than just words that represent, discourse forms objects and concepts by bounding how they can be thought of, talked about and acted upon. Discourse orders the world of things. In talking about psychiatric discourses, Foucault (1972) stated:

> [D]iscourse finds a way of limiting its domain, of defining what it is talking about, of giving it the status of an object—and therefore of making it manifest, nameable, and describable. (p. 41)

These discourses are produced and instantiated, or re-performed, as knowledge at the level of practice, action and text. Knowledge and truth, in this conceptualization, are constructed and institutionalized through practice and the coordination of material objects. There are a multiplicity of discourses (e.g., medical discourses, science discourses, legal discourses) that circulate within social spaces; they may even merge to create new discourses (e.g., sexuality or psychiatry discourses).

The institutionalization of discourse, or knowledge, as power is an important dimension of Foucault's work. Unlike social theorists who have argued that knowledge is defined by those holding economic and social power (e.g., Karl Marx, Emile Durkheim), he inverted the idea of a sovereign concept of power (i.e., a premise that power can be owned similar to a commodity) to argue that power is an effect of and constituted by knowledge, and vice versa. Foucault (1978) rejected the premise that individuals wield power to control and impose their will. Instead, he reconceptualized the constructs of power and knowledge, as well as their relationship, to argue that power is a "complex strategical situation" (p. 93) that both produces knowledge as well as is, itself, an effect of knowledge. In framing knowledge as situational, he emphasized the multiplicity of social relations (i.e., knowledge and mechanisms) that converge to enact knowledge. He interjected a spatial dimension in knowledge production as it was envisioned as an act, or practice, that is mobilized by a wide array of spatially dispersed and buttressing discursive and material relations.

The Role of Practices and Technologies in Knowledge Production

The concept of practice surfaces over and over again in various social theories, ranging from Althusser, Pierre Bourdieu (1990) to Foucault. The place of practices within the production of knowledge is central in this reconceptualization of knowledge production and warrants more elaboration. An extended discussion of what constitutes practices will help us to define more precisely how we will talk about them in this project. However, the discussion of practices needs to be carried out with a discussion of the material world. Practices are carried out in a world of objects. We locate the world of things by framing them as technologies and as enmeshed in knowledge.

Foucault's emphasis on multiple converging relations in knowledge production relies on practices as the catalyst for integrating relationships. We align ourselves with this argument and refer to practices as the enunciative, or signifying, acts that individuals engage in through bodily actions. These can be routines or rituals in which the body is positioned as a result of institutional knowledge. The body is disciplined and governed to enact particular practices within particular contexts. Talk, too, should be seen as a practice, specifically expert talk. Articulating the truths about an object or an entity is an effect of knowledge and material relationships. Similar to

Althusser's concept of interpellation of ideology, expert talk is an act of discourse summoning an individual and vice versa. The convergence and mobilization of spatial relationships (i.e., institutionally recognized discourse-knowledge, material apparatuses, physical edifices or buildings) facilitates the production of truth statements, or what has been termed the incitement of practices (Butler, 1999). Individuals take up discourses to practice what Foucault (1980) terms régimes of truth. Discourse recruits bodies to construct objects, worldviews, and norms of engagement. He clarifies this in stating:

> What makes power hold good, what makes it accepted, is simply the fact that it doesn't only weigh on us as a force that says no, but that it traverses and produces things, it induces pleasure, forms knowledge, produces discourse. (p. 119)

Hence, knowledge and power are enacted through practice. They not only prohibit particular actions, or as Foucault notes "as a force that says no," but incite particular embodied practices (e.g., talk and action).

The force of knowledge through practices is incomplete without the coordination of material relations. Technologies, as material objects, always come into play within institutional contexts. However, technologies are integrated into practices by knowledge. Embodied practices impose order upon objects and structural relations to work within the logic of the reigning knowledge. Nicholas Rose (1996) builds on Foucault's theorizing of this nexus to posit a concept of technologies that encapsulates these attributes. He defines technologies as:

> Any assembly structured by a practical rationality governed by a more or less conscious goal. Human technologies are hybrid assemblages of knowledges, instruments, persons, systems of judgment, buildings and spaces, underpinned at the programmatic level by certain presuppositions and objectives about human beings. (p. 26)

The emphasis on the integration of bodies, instruments and knowledges in this conceptualization of technologies is what draws us to this definition. The amalgamation of objects and knowledges suggests an interplay, or what might be seen as a trialectical relationship, between a multitude of relations. The trialectical relationship that is formed through this interaction and integration has an inherent spatial element and openness that is not found in the highly temporal ordering of the thesis-antithesis-synthesis logic found in dialectical reasoning (Lefebvre, 1991; Soja, 1996). Within this trialectical reasoning, technologies can still be shaping elements within a field of relations but not necessarily determinative ones, as in Marxian or some non-conflict oriented structuralist theories. The logic underpinning a material object, or structure, can function to orient other technologies as they interact, yet their force is contingent upon the nexus of the presuppositions and objectives (i.e., knowledge/discourse) of the interconnecting technologies.

Space and Spatialized and Spatializing Practices

Our explanation of the integration of knowledge and technologies through embodied practices has alluded to a spatial dimension (i.e., spatial relations) that we have not fully discussed thus far. Space is an important element in discussing knowledge, technologies and practices. These three are all spatial, that is, occurring amongst relations. However, prior to discussing spatial knowledge, technologies and practices, we need to outline key attributes of space that underpin our conceptualization of it. We specifically draw from the theorizing of Henri Lefebvre, Edward Soja, and Michel Foucault.

First, space is not an object that exists emptily waiting for something to fill it. It is, rather, something that is produced. That is, human (i.e., bodily) processes of production come to play in making space. Lefebvre (1991) recognized that this is an odd premise in stating, "To speak of 'producing space' sounds bizarre, so great is the sway still held by the ideal that empty space is prior to whatever ends up filling it" (p. 15). Second, space is produced through practices, specifically spatial practices. All three theorists– Foucault, Lefebvre, Soja–see the everyday practices of life as the primary locus of spatial production. These embodied acts, Lefebvre (1991) notes, "secrete that society's space" (p. 38). Lastly, these spatial practices involve both knowledge and material relations, or what we have discussed as technologies. Spatial practices involve knowledge in the form of established understandings and ideology. This knowledge, or what Lefebvre (1991) and Soja (1996) refer to as representations of space, works at the level of how individuals and collectives imagine and talk about space. This may manifest in the form of numbers, signs, or other verbal forms. This conceptualization of knowledge in spatial production adheres to the properties of discourse articulated in Foucault's theory of régimes of truth.

The material world of technologies also has an important role in the production of space as it interplays with knowledge. Technologies are inherently spatial. They are enacted, or coordinated, to produce networks of spatial relations between objects. Through the forging of these relations, technologies function as spatialized and spatializing objects. The former refers to the positioning of objects spatially whereas the latter suggests processes of coordinating ensuing technologies that are encountered so that they, too, are brought into a spatial knowledge and relations. Rob Shields (1997) elaborates on the spatializing piece of this in stating:

> 'Social spatialization' names the situation which… is not just a question of 'Space' but of overlaid 'Spaces' which are made up of multitudinous 'places,' good and bad (the 'right' and 'wrong' side 'of the tracks', 'dangerous' urban areas, ghettos, 'middle class enclaves', public squares, private yards, the sanctified space of a cathedral, the proface space of a tavern). (p. 190)

Both process (i.e., actions) and form (configuration of objects and relations) are constituted, or produced, and reconstituted, or re-produced, through the enactment of spatial practices. The meaning of objects and the relationship between them are delineated as spatial practices are repeated and canonized as truth.

Two Examples

A way to move this explanation from the abstract to the concrete is to describe a common situation where knowledge, practices, technologies, and space converge and are produced. Foucault makes this nexus transparent in showing how particular knowledge, technologies, practices and spaces came together around sexuality and madness to make them historically visible and, ultimately, manageable. In the case of sexuality, he argued that a variety of knowledge and technologies converged in the form of social texts, such as professional medical manuals and political-religious pronouncements, as well as embodied practices, such as the confessional-type examination, to 'will to scientific knowledge' a particular discourse and space of sexuality. The practices and knowledge of a multitude of technical and professional agents as well as medical and university institutions overlapped to construct matrices of professional medical interpretations that codified what individuals uttered in the rituals of examination. These divergent entities and knowledges converged spatially to form a network of relations that resulted in a knowledge, or régime of truth, of 'normal' and 'abnormal' sexuality. A practice, knowledge, and space of difference emerged as a pathology of sexual deviancies, as well as subjects, was produced that did not exist prior to the 19th century. The spaces of clinics and brothels became further defined and differentiated from other spaces as experts, patients, and clients routinely engaged in practices to attend to and manage the constructed differences of 'the pervert' and the sexually 'normal.' Over time and through the production of space, the productive and arbitrary qualities of these imagined differentiations have been lost as they have become naturalized, or viewed as real, through spatial practices.

This discussion of the role of overlapping spatial relations (i.e., knowledge, technologies, and practices) to construct a knowledge and technology of differentiation is not isolated to the social sciences. The second example that we offer points to similar processes that Foucault has described but that are located in the laboratory work of physicists and chemists (cf., Hacking, 1992; Latour & Woolgar, 1979). Where some of these, such as Bruno Latour and Steve Woolgar's (1979) work, have focused on the practices and dispositions involved in the social construction of scientific knowledge, others have sought to name and understand how machines, knowledge and practices function to shape the epistemic outlook of experts to make differentiations in reality. For example, Karen Knorr Cetina (1999) provides a cogent explanation of how the machinery of the laboratory has functioned in processes of knowledge production of particle physicists and molecular biologists. She argues that the construction of knowledge in these fields is not only an outcome of routines and practices but also a mechanical one, involving machines, that shapes what and how scientists know. She shows how the laboratory machinery (e.g., particle detectors, super computers, Large Haldron Colliders) of physicists and molecular biologists do not merely open up a view of reality, but involve processes of "reconfiguring" the natural into new signs. In discussing this reconfiguration of nature she states:

> I have associated laboratories with the notion of reconfiguration, with the setting-up of an order in laboratories that is built upon upgrading the ordinary and mundane components of social life. Laboratories *recast* objects of investigation by inserting them into new temporal and territorial regimes. They play upon these objects' natural rhythms and developmental possibilities, bring them together in new numbers, renegotiate their sizes, and redefine their internal makeup. (Cetina, 1999, p. 43)

Cetina's focus on the technologies that recast objects as something other than their natural state does not depart too far from the writings of Foucault.

The scientist and her machinery are part of the "epistemic culture" (Cetina, 1999)–one of knowledge, practices, and technologies–in which she is embedded. Her expertise is entangled in an array of spatial relations comprised of "different architectures of empirical approaches, specific constructions of the referent, particular ontologies of instruments, and different social machines" (Cetina 1999, p. 3). Cetina suggests that our ability to access and name an unmediated reality is ever more distant.

To summarize the conceptual framing of the analytical units that we employ in the examination of the production of the East Side, West Side and Central City school and student, we have defined knowledge as discursive acts that are effects of multiple converging relations. These relations include knowledge, itself, and material technologies that have a historical element yet that are mobilized through practice. Practices, meanwhile, involve the bodily acts (i.e., verbal and non-verbal) of enacting knowledge. They locate the body within particular discourses, or, to state this differently, inscribe the body with particular social orderings of what it is, what it can do and be, or what has been termed subjectivities (Hall, 1997; McCarthy & Crichlow, 1993). As knowledge and practices are enacted, space is produced. Space encompasses a network of spatial relations that is produced as knowledge (i.e., discourses) and technologies are assembled through practices. These three realms come together to constitute how meanings, identities, and practices are constructed.

The Contingency of Knowledge Production

Where analyses such as Foucault's (1978) and Cetina's (1999) suggest that we find ourselves in some sense of a cyborg state (Haraway, 1991)–that is, in a hybrid state of machine and organism, or a creature of social reality as well as a construction of human fiction–the participation of individuals within an architecture of different relations complicates matters, however. Spatial relations, or what Cetina refers to as architectures, are not completely fixed. Many have suggested that the social position of individuals as members of intersecting racial, classed, and gendered communities render unstable and contingent the spatial relations that constitute the field of production (Hall, 1997; hooks, 1990 McCarthy, 1998; Soja, 1996). To state this differently, because domination (i.e., power) can be theorized, in part, as a spatial situation of converging relations, individuals' movement and interaction across different relationships (e.g., knowledges, material entities) has the potential to open up other knowledges, ways of being, and practices. The configuration of a field of spatial relations that produces particular ontologies, concepts, and spaces can be disturbed and potentially reworked to produce other imaginings of self, other, and space (see Bhabha, 1994; Dolby, 2001; McCarthy, 1998). Yet, historical configurations of different spatial-social relations are not completely up for grabs. Historical configurations of material relations and knowledge can facilitate the articulation of a particular architecture. The effect is the production of familiar patterns in the formation of knowledges, subjects, and social spaces.

Space, Knowledge, and Practice as Trialectically Constituted

The relationship that we are drawing between space, knowledge, practice is one that envisions these as mutually constituting. Particularly, we want to frame these within Soja's concept of a trialectic. Trialectical reasoning is a way of envisioning relationships that avoids seeking to create hierarchies, or neatly accounting for central units. It also rejects the dualisms that have plagued dialectical reasoning. The realm of the social is seen as a messy place of a multitude of relationships, a premise consistent with the idea of spatial relationships. It leaves room for what Lefebvre (1991) has termed as an 'Other,' or what Soja (1996) refers to Thirdspaces. As a result, it provides a framework of relationality that is able to account for complexity, the co-mingling of multiple entities, objects, and knowledges, and, most importantly, the spatial dimensions of knowledge and practice.

To elaborate on this, let us turn to Edward Soja's (1996) work around the trialectics of being and space in discussing the production of other identities, knowledges, and spaces. In his book *Thirdspace: Journeys to Los Angeles and Other Real-and-Imagined Places*, he reads across the landscape of work of different feminist and postcolonial scholars using the interpretive lens of the Thirdspace that he draws from Henri Lefebvre. He specifically examines the work of bell hooks, Cynthia Hooper, Gloria Anzaldua, Gayatri Spivak, and Edward Said, among others, in order to show how new, or "Other," real-and-imagined spaces and conceptions of self are named as "possibilities for a new cultural politics of difference and identity" (hooks in Soja, 1996, p. 96) in a process of trialectical reasoning. Soja's reading of these works focuses on the manner in which new selves, knowledges, and spaces are envisioned and practiced as these authors re-define home spaces, the borders, and the borderlands. He identifies how they rework the spheres of the Firstspace, or the analytical (e.g., quantitative or diagrammed) readings of physical space, and the Secondspace, the domain of conceptual space or representations of space, to produce what he defines as the Thirdspace, or the lived, which encompasses the First and Second space. This Thirdspace is a social positioning, an epistemological standpoint, and what we have termed here as spatial relations that radically rework ontological and epistemological conceptions (i.e., Firstspace and Secondspace) to form what Soja and Lefebvre term "an-Other." Soja explains this:

> *Thirdspace epistemologies* can now be briefly re-described as arising from the sympathetic deconstruction and heuristic reconstitution of the Firstspace-Secondspace duality, another example of what I have called thirding-as-Othering. Such thirding is designed not just to critique Firstspace and Secondspace modes of thought, but also to reinvigorate their approaches to spatial knowledge with new possibilities heretofore unthought of inside the traditional spatial disciplines. (p. 81)

A concrete description of how Soja conceptualizes this Thirdspace may be helpful in further clarifying this concept. A description of how he sees bell hooks enacting the Thirdspace may be helpful. Soja identifies hooks' (1990) discussion in *Yearning: Race, gender, and cultural politics* of home space and choosing the margins as a space from which to theorize as an example of the 'radical opening-up' of new spaces of self, knowing, and resistance. He reads hooks as theorizing in a trialectical framework as she re-envisions historicality, sociality, and spatiality—the elements of his trialectics of being. The spatial terms (i.e., margin, center, home) that she evokes, he states, entangle in new ways the geographical, epistemological, and historical. He sees her practicing a self that is transgressive, in that she is, at times, "simultaneously central and marginal (and purely neither at the same time)" (p. 97). Hooks' movement between and integration of spatial relations facilitates a new space of knowledges, selves, and political alignments. He states:

> [hooks'] evocative process of choosing marginality reconceptualizes the problematic of subjection by deconstructing and reordering both margin and center. In those restructured and recentered margins, new spaces of opportunity and action are created, the new spaces that difference makes. For hooks, and by extension and invitation, all others involved in this spatial disordering of difference, there is a "definite distinction between the marginality which is imposed by oppressive structure and that marginality one chooses as site of resistance, as location of radical openness and possibility. (Soja, 1996, p. 98)

What becomes important for our purposes is how Soja bundles different concepts of spatiality and beingness in order to recognize the contingency and disruption that emerges as different relationships are mobilized. Trialectical reasoning allows him to discuss different domains to theorize their mutual constitution. Furthermore, he, as well as us, is excited by the contingency that different communities can incite as they rework the conceived (Firstspace), perceived (Secondspace), and lived (Thirdspace)—elements of the trialectics of spatiality. Moments of alternative knowledge become possible as the deconstruction and reconstitution of the trialectics of spatiality and being are put into motion.

Space, Knowledge, and Practice

This chapter has provided a detailed explanation of the central theoretical units that we employ in this examination of "West Side," "East Side" and "Central City" students and schools. The conceptualization of knowledge, technologies, practices and space that we have aligned ourselves with departs from the enlightenment framings that have historically anchored these constructs. We have sought to position these units in a relationship where they are envisioned as social, historical, mutually constituted and somewhat open to disruption. The metaphors that underpin this relationship include terms such as interplay and relationality.

What follows in Chapter 3 is a history of the East Side and West Side constructs within the space of the city. We analyze the meanings circulated by the local media and local politicians of these spaces and those who reside there to show how the social existence of these constructs precedes the present. We show how these constructs have come to historically signify particular meanings about race and class.

CHAPTER 3

HISTORICAL FORMATION OF A GEOGRAPHICAL DIVIDE

The conceptual framework that we described in Chapter 2 prompts us to trace the knowledge of the East Side, West Side and Central City school and student to spatial relationships that expand beyond the walls of schools and to historical moments that precede the present. This knowledge is intertwined with the spatial relationships (i.e., people and physical elements) of the city as well as the cultural meanings that residents, city leaders and the media employed, and currently employ, to name and talk about these spaces and entities. Constructs such as the "East Side" and the "West Side" have a life in practice that precedes the present. The 'past' of such knowledge shapes the present, yet the past is over-run, at times, by the present. Randal Kennedy (2002), among others, has made this argument in demonstrating how the construct "Nigger" has historically held some of its semantic coherence over the course of time, while at the same time that its meaning has been inverted from a negative term to a positive one in different settings. The analysis that we provide here parallels, in some senses, Kennedy's study of the word Nigger and Foucault's examination of sexuality, in that it is premised on the idea that the West Side and the East Side constructs are socially constructed knowledge. Each construct has been and is currently being rewritten with propositions–many of them uttered before–of where the West Side and the East Side geographically lie, who belongs there, and what transpires in these spaces.

What follows is a description of the physical space of Salt Valley City and some of the historical discursive practices that have been part of these spaces. This description of the physical becomes important as we discuss the convergence of conceived space and the knowledge, or meanings, that come to describe the inhabitants of these spaces. Furthermore, this description and analysis will help us to assert that the constructs of the West Side and the East Side are socio-historical units that have a presence in the past as denoting racial and classed difference. We then provide a historical mapping of the public life of the West Side and East Side constructs as they were employed in the media during the period of 1900-2000. We show how the West Side has come to be underpinned by overtly racialized and criminalizing meanings, whereas the East Side has existed, for the most, in a precarious silence, with a few intonations, at times, of a pastoral space. Alongside examining the dominant knowledge of the East Side and West Side, this chapter also contextualizes this production with a description of the structural organization of the city. Specifically, it explains how patterns in the organization of the city's built environment and occupational (i.e., social class) dimensions also follow a racial and class oriented logic.

The Historical Landscape of the City

Salt Valley City is tucked between the foothills of the Wasatch Mountain range and a patchwork of desert tundra and white, salt marshes that lead up to the Great Salt Lake. Houses that range in cost from the millions to the hundreds of thousand dollars are situated up and around the rim of the eastern and northern lying foothills. This area is commonly referred to by locals as the "the East Side" or "the benches." As you travel westward, down the foothills toward the Great Salt Lake, other East Side neighborhoods begin, still located on the benches, that are composed of houses priced in the two to three hundred thousand dollar range. This residential area has a mix of upscale sidewalk cafés and restaurants that are couched between residences.

A central thoroughfare for the city divides the benches to mark the beginning of two other neighborhoods, known by those who reside there as the Central City and Green Park neighborhoods. The only visual marker denoting this area as such is a community center with the sign "The Central City Community Center." The costs of houses in this flat area drops significantly in comparison to property on the benches. As you move westward, this neighborhood gradually gives way to the downtown area that is composed of a mixture of remodeled Victorian houses, strip malls, a Mormon temple square, and skyscrapers. On the edge of this part of the city sit living remnants of the past with the Greek Orthodox Church and the Japanese-American Christian Church as well as the Japanese-American Buddhist Temple, the only remains of what used to be "Japan-town." As you continue westward, the downtown is abruptly cut off by a maze of railroad spurs and a railroad yard that were constructed at the turn of the twentieth century. Industrial buildings are interspersed in between the spurs, as well as a two block area that is the primary area for the city's homeless shelters. Across the street from the shelters lies the city's recent development project aimed at "gentrifying" this area, which includes a multiple level outdoor mega-mall, named Gateway, that houses upscale retail shops. The mall is surrounded by expensive, newly constructed neo/art deco style condominiums marketed at young singles and professionals.

Just a few blocks westward a multi-acre train yard further dissects the city. More heavy industry oriented buildings and older businesses can be found within the train track lines as well as various ethnic supermarkets, such as *La Michoacana-Productos de Mexico*, whose presence preceded the gentrification project. An elevated freeway that runs north-south parallels the central railroad lines that cut the city in half. It marks, for many city residents, the beginning of another neighborhood, commonly referred to by locals as the "West Side." Houses that are larger (i.e., building square footage and lot size) than those on the other side of the freeway, yet markedly less expensive, are situated between the freeway and the airport. Many of these are new developments of mass produced tract housing that are sold relatively cheaply. The airport marks the border of the city as it opens up to the marshes of the Great Salt Lake. Within this neighborhood, a mix of ethnic restaurants, primarily Mexican, and convenience stores are intermixed with various fast food chains, strip malls with dollar discount stores and major chain supermarkets. The area is interspersed with both large and small churches, some dating back to the turn of the twentieth century while others show the markings of new construction. Many of the business and church storefront signs are written in English, Spanish, or Tongan.

While the current geography reflects the recent growth in the Latino/Mexican and Tongan/Pacific Islander population, as well as the physical disconnect of the predominately white, middle-class from these communities, these spatial relationships need to be placed within a historical context of housing patterns as well as the patterns of discourses surrounding these spaces in order to understand their present state.

Prior to the arrival of Europeans to the Utah area in the eighteenth century, the region that is currently the Salt Valley was inhabited by the Fremont, Ute, Northern Shoshone, Goshute and Paiute peoples (May, 1987; McPherson, 2000). In 1847, the Mormons arrived by wagon train and deemed the valley Zion, the sacred site referred to in the Book of Mormon (Arrington & Davis, 1979; Vogel, 1986). A discourse of the "Other" was already at work in their social frameworks prior to encountering the Indian people of the Salt Valley region. The Book of Mormon stated that Mormons would encounter within the land of Zion a group of people, termed "Lamanites," that were at one time enlightened people who had fallen from the grace of God. These people, the Mormon scripture held, were given dark skin by God as a result of their fallen spiritual status, and were awaiting spiritual renewal (May, 1987; McPherson, 2000; Vogel, 1986). The Ute, Shoshone and others were enveloped in this discourse. By the mid-1850s, the droves of white settlers outnumbered the native peoples of the area. The dual forces of missionary work and annihilation were set in motion.

In the center of the region, Salt Valley City became the central port of entry for white settlers. The city had a population of 8,000 inhabitants prior to the completion of the transcontinental railroad lines, pre-1868 (McCormick, 2000). The city was comprised of white Mormon settlers, a handful of black Mormons who came over on the first wagon trains, and a small number of Chinese and Mexican immigrants who were employees of the first railroad company. The settlers removed the Utes, Goshutes and Shoshone tribes from this area a few years after their arrival, placing them on reservations in various isolated parts of the city (Defa, 2000; May, 1987). Once the rail line from the east coast to the west was complete, the city grew quickly to around 45,000 inhabitants as gold miners, who never made it to California, and railroad workers made Salt Valley City their home (McCormick, 2000).

The racial and class divisions within the city's geographical layout crystallized from the onset of its development. As white Mormon settlers staked out land on the rising slopes of what was to become the eastern section of the city, they relegated other racial groups to the peripheries of the city. Chinese residents were segregated to a one block perimeter on the western edge of the city that came to be known as Plum Alley, not too far from the railroad tracks (May 1987). The tenement houses in this two block area were intermixed with saloons, hotels, and brothels. Plum Alley took the form of Salt Valley City's "Chinatown" as Chinese males engaged in everyday practices such as gathering in Chinese operated tea rooms, gambling houses, and restaurants (McCormick, 2000). Meanwhile, the small number of black settlers who migrated with the first wave of settlers resided, for a period of 30 or so years, on the southern edge of the city (Coleman, 1980). Many purchased property in this section of the city and created a space of activity and interaction for the small black community. By the turn of the twentieth century, Greek, Japanese, Russian Jews, and Mexican immigrants began to arrive by train to seek out land and fortunes in silver mining. Finding a place to call home, however, would be their first task.

The designation of livable spaces for the newly arrived ethnic and racial groups were caught up in the City Council's decisions regarding land use

(McCormick, 2000). The designation of desirable and undesirable spaces were determined as local politicians carved up the city into residential, business, and industrial space. Ultimately, these decisions would contribute to the making of the East Side and West Side constructs and spaces. At the heart of these policies, were decisions involving the expansion of the railroad track lines, or railroad spurs, into the western edge of the city. Railroad companies and city industrialists lobbied the city to create an industrial area that would allow the trains to access city warehouses that would be built as soon as tracks were laid. The plan permitted hundreds of railroad spurs to dissect the western edge of the city to create a noticeable divide that was marked by the presence and movement of trains (McCormick, 2000). The lots that were left to the west side of the tracks, mostly large farming lots owned by white, working class Mormons, were sold either to businessmen seeking to create warehouses by the newly established railroad spurs or were divided into smaller lots that were sold to create tenement houses. Warehouses soon replaced what had been farmland and empty lots. Patches of industrial use property were created that were bustling with the noise and pollution from the train and wagon traffic.

The division, or honeycombing, of lots into smaller land tracts, and the placement of railroad tracks did not result in a concentrated industrial center, however. Large, multi-room buildings were also wedged between the web of spurs, warehouses, and lumberyards to create a multiple-use space. While the white Mormon and Catholic populations inhabited the lots on the east side of Main Street, away from the trains and congestion, racial housing covenants propelled Greek, Japanese, Syrian, and Chinese immigrants to move into, and were relegated to, the buildings next to and within the spurs of tracks to create small ethnic colonies within the larger community (Papanikolas, 1976). Chinese newcomers were drawn, as well as forced by the white population, to the already established city block known as Plum Alley. Other ethnic groups rented cheap housing within the noisy, dusty and compressed industrial area to create separate ethnic enclaves that successively lined the west side of the railroad tracks. For example, the Japanese-American community established an area of the city that was just a few blocks away from Plum Alley, which they termed *Nihonjin Machi*. Translated, this means "Japanese town" (Moriyasu, 1996). This three block area was home to Japanese-American businesses ranging from florists, hotels, fish markets, to the Japanese Buddhist and Christian churches. The Italian community, or what locals termed "Little Italy," neighbored *Nihonjin Machi*. Next to the

Italian owned grocery stores, saloons and restaurants followed the Greek section of the city, another extensively developed ethnic neighborhood, similar in size to *Nihonjin Machi*. It was a concentrated area of three area blocks with over thirty buildings housing Greek style coffeehouses, saloons, bakeries, a pharmacy, and grocery stores (Papanikolas, 1976). All of these enclaves were in one way or another adjoining or in between the railroad spurs and the area zoned as industrial. Most importantly, they were all also situated on the western edge of the city.

Where the city's designation of an industrial space partly facilitated the establishment of ethnic communities, the city and the media further sealed the placement of these communities to a West Side that was separate from the white community, as well as ushered in the spatial construct of 'West Side' into the citizenry's imagination by establishing the spatial zone the "business district." By 1908, the construct of a "business district" was introduced into the public's parlance by the city council. The spatial parameters of this business district were drawn and communicated to the public by the media. The *Evening Telegram* reported on November 13, 1908, that the saloon district would be further defined and bound, and explicitly introduced the term "business district" to its readers by setting it off with quotations:

> The present "business" district of Salt Lake is contained in that part of the city between Fourth South and North Temple and Second East and South Temple and Second South, leading to depots. This district has been established by the city council in issuing licenses to peddlers. (Telegram, November 13, 1908, p. 1)

The establishment and identification of a section of the city termed the business district is an important event in the creation of the constructs of an East and West Side. First, this act ensured that the ethnic residential communities would not physically merge with the white residential areas. There would be no eventual physical joining of these spaces through the expansion of middle-class housing developments that ethnic communities could slowly move into. The space between the ethnic and white communities would be comprised of businesses, rendering impossible spontaneous conversation and interaction between these communities. Second, it also conceptually created a center within the city, and within the imaginary of the city's citizenry. With the City Council and the media designating the business district as the center, city residents seemed to have begun at this point to use it as a reference point to geographically make distinctions between the neighborhoods west and east of the business district. In other words, as the business district was defined as the center of commerce, a discourse of an East Side and a West Side emerged to describe those other spaces that buttressed the space socially defined as the center of the city.

Historical Practices of the West Side and East Side

While the noise and movement of the trains and the concentration of ethnic and racial communities deemed the neighborhoods to the west of the downtown as the least desirable area for the white population to reside, other discursive and bodily practices would further codify this area so that it attained meanings as a "dangerous" place and its inhabitants as "criminal." For instance, the city facilitated the centralization of its criminal and "unruly" elements by locating the city's houses of prostitution to the area next to the Chinese quarter of the city. White Mormons, who owned property on Commercial Street, the street next to Plum Alley, leased buildings to local madams who established parlor houses on this block (McCormick, 2000). At the same time, the city also designated this area as "soap box corner" for the city's socialist contingency. Between 1910 and 1930, the city confined the gathering of the city's Socialists, Anarchists, and Wobblies to the area populated by Chinese immigrants and sex workers and their clients. Union leaders such as Joe Hill of the IWW as well as religious leaders, such as William Thurston Brown from the Unitarian Church, would turn this space into a populist pulpit. Hence, practices of criminal behavior and social activism by white residents who would venture into this area for the sake of pleasure or protest would give this space a particular connotation.

The meanings that city leaders tied to the space where its ethnic community inhabited became more transparent as the city contemplated moving the brothels that were located next to Chinatown. In these discussions, early manifestations of the discourse of deficiency as well as the West Side construct surfaced. What prompted this talk and activity were the complaints of Salt Valley City businessmen as well as the Mormon clergy to city officials that the red light district was too close to the business district and the temple. The mayor at that time, John S. Bransford, responded to the complaints by contacting a local madam, Belle London. Bransford urged her to purchase a property away from the business district and move the trade to another part of the city. Madam Belle, whose real name was Dora P. Topham, purchased, with the city's help, a city block right in the middle of the Greek community. Madam London followed the city police chief's instructions and had the city architect design an enclosed compound. Three years later, in 1911, she completed the construction on a four walled compound (McCormick, 2000; Nichols, 2002). In explaining the decision to relocate the brothel to the Greek community, Mayor Bransford disclosed the racial and classed discourses that were beginning to crystallize as knowledge around this space and its residents. He stated publicly, "We found that most of the better class of residents were leaving the area anyway because of the influx of Italians and Greeks who live in that neighborhood" (McCormick, 2000, p. 118).

While a discourse of a better class and lower class group of people framed decisions about the uses of city space, an early manifestation of the West Side construct also emerged in the talk of city residents as civic and political groups objected to the movement of the brothel. Their choice of language to note its place of relocation provides us with a purview of how a space called West Side was beginning to crystallize. In its early uses, the construct is strictly a spatial reference, pointing to a particular geographical locale. For instance, the leadership of the local American Party penned a letter to one of the city's newspapers objecting to the process and plan pertaining to the move of the city's brothels, as well as the media's depiction of this political group using the spatial referent West Side:

> Owing to the fact that the American party managers have been unable to procure a place on the west side of the city, where a meeting could be held to emphasize the position of the American administration in regard to the establishment of a red light district on that side of the city, no public declaration has been made, and it now appearing [sic] that the Smoot "Mouth" and News have voiced the infamous and lying charges that the officials of the present administration favor the establishment of a red light district on the west side of the city. (The Salt Lake Tribune, November 1, 1908).

The designation of a "west side" in statements such as these shows how a spatial division was beginning to emerge in the view of residents. Moreover, this space starts to become officially inscribed, through processes of inscription in the media, as a place of criminal and immoral behavior.

These were not the only pejorative statements in public circulation at this time. The discourse linking criminality, morality and race could be found in other public statements being made about this area in local newspapers. John McCormick (2000) reports that between 1903 and 1925 the *Salt Lake Tribune* continuously described Commercial Street and Plum Alley as "a resort of gamblers and fast women" (p. 97). Ten years later, the *Deseret News*, among other daily newspapers, still referred to the occupants of this area using terms such as "the demi-monde, the male parasite, the dope fiend, the gambler, and the beggar" (McCormick, 2000, p. 97). The early period of the city witnessed a project of constructing racial difference through language about people as well as place. Prior to examining the discourses of the inhabitants of particular parts of the city, as well as the space itself, that were in circulation during the latter part of the twentieth century, we turn to the realm of the city's structural (i.e., material) relations.

Residential Space

While particular discourses began to cohere to produce meanings of the people who lived on the West Side of the city, as well as of the West Side place itself, the organization of the city's structural relations, particularly its housing patterns, also followed the logic of a race and class division. The residential areas of the various ethnic communities during the period of 1890 through 1930 were contained between the business district and the railroad yard. The city's white population was either to the east of the city's business center or were located in rural areas west of the city's development (McCormick, 2000).

These spatial boundaries remained intact, for the most, up until the 1980s. For example, even though the ethnic population was relatively small in comparison to other major cities, Harvey Kantor's (2004) analysis of census tract data of Salt Valley City depicts a narrative of continuous segregation in the city's housing patterns along the lines of race and class. He found that in 1960 the only section of the city to have 10 percent or more of its population identify as non-white was the area between the railroad yard and the Greek and Italian sections of the city, or the area historically defined as the west side. The sections neighboring this roughly five block area also showed a segment of non-white residents that ranged between 5 and 10 percent of its population.

By 1980, Salt Valley City's population experienced a significant increase (>5000/group) in the number of Pacific Islanders (i.e., Tongans), Latina/os (i.e., Mexicans) and Asians (i.e., Laotians and Vietnamese) (Utah Office of Planning and Budget, 1989). The same two geographical areas where most non-whites have historically resided witnessed a jump in their numbers where their composition was roughly 20 percent or more of the population. Kantor's (2004) analysis shows Latina/o, Pacific Islander and Asian residents moving to other parts of the city by 1980. This movement is primarily farther west, in the area between the north-south running freeway and the city's airport. The white families who resided in these areas fled to the suburbs that lied south and north of the city, a pattern that began in the 1950s (Kantor, 2004).

The population residing on the West Side of the city has also been primarily working class. In 1930, the inhabitants of the various ethnic enclaves that lined the western edge of the city were primarily employed in mining, service work, or some other type of heavy labor (McCormick, 2000; Papanikolas, 1976). The social economic status of the residents of this part of the city holds steady through the twentieth century as census data tracked at least 20 (1960) to 40 (2000) percent of the residents employed as either laborers or machinery operators (Kantor, 2004; U.S. Census Bureau, 2003).

The area defined as the East Side, or benches, also remained constant in its racial and class composition. At no time in history do the numbers of non-whites in this part of the city exceed more than 10 percent. Furthermore, a steady pattern holds for this area where at least 40 percent of its residents have occupations that are classified as either professional, managerial or technical in nature (Kantor, 2004). To put this another way, the city's class relations also adhered to a racial division where educational attainment and high paying jobs were divided along race lines.

The technologies and practices that facilitated the creation of this residential segregation did not differ from other metropolitan areas in the US (see Massey & Denton, 1993; Jackson, 1985; Meyer, 2000). White residents and realtors institutionalized discriminatory practices by enforcing mechanisms such as racially restrictive covenants that forbade owners to sell their properties to non-whites (Kantor, 2004; McCormick, 2000). With the Supreme Court deeming these practices unenforceable in 1948, the market then worked to maintain the West Side/East Side color and class line by pushing the cost of properties on the benches beyond the reach of the working class (Kantor, 2004). The racial stratification of labor within the city meant that even if racially restrictive covenants were not in place, most people of color did not have the economic resources to purchase property on the East Side of the city.

Contemporary Media Constructions of the West Side and East Side

While a racial and class division solidified in the built environment of the city, the racial and classed overtones have remained at the core of the meanings of the West Side, as well as a precarious silence about the East Side throughout the latter part of the twentieth century. The media as well as local politicians have generally represented the former using language such as "dirty," "prone to crime," "foreign" and residing illegally in the US These meanings have not departed greatly in tone from the earlier references to the "demi-monde" and the "lesser-classed" that city leaders and newspapers employed during the early part of the 1900s. They still adhere to the local and national discourse of deficiency and criminality that has been repeatedly deployed to characterize African-Americans and immigrants (Kennedy, 2002; Perea, 1997). What has changed over the course of the last fifty years, however, is the way that these meanings have been attached to the spatial construct West Side. A pattern has emerged in the city's newspapers and the statements of politicians where these discourses go hand-in-hand with this spatial construct. What is notable about this pairing is that, first, the West Side has spatially reached the status of place. No longer do residents refer to this part of the city as the "West Side of the city," but, instead, simply say West Side. Secondly, the meanings attached to the residents who live in this space have been collapsed in the term West Side. That is, the term denotes an ontology of the residents who live there as well as a sense of place.

Two examples provide a general description of the way that language is structured to convey this line of reasoning. The first is a contemporary news story that bears the headline, "When junk starts piling up in the yard, property values start going down" (Baltezore, 1996, D3). The article describes how the "accumulated junk" in West Side residents' yards has become a plight, and that such junk invites criminals. The individuals interviewed deploy the West Side signifier to geographically locate a sense of place. The article states, "Since taking office in 1994, [City Council member] Lee has waged a relentless battle to get Westside homeowners in his District 1 to clean up their properties." Just a few lines down from this, a statement from the city's chief prosecutor follows that couples the construct West Side to criminal behavior. She states, "That kind of blight seems to be an invitation to criminals to the Westside–it gives the impression that neighbors don't care. Drug houses tend to be in homes where the standard of conduct is not up to code. Dealers are putting their energies into running the drug business and not keeping up the house."

The second example is a newspaper article with a headline "Westside anger" (Loomis, 2000). The article describes the resentment of a community council member from the west side region of the city after the city council rejected plans to locate a mall in the area. The newspaper quotes the councilman as stating, "Salt Lake City's Westside needs more English speaking stores. We're tired of all this Spanish speaking stuff coming in. I can't read the names on the doors. It's starting to look like Tijuana in my area." While the article closes with statements by Latino community leaders voicing their concerns over the councilman's views, the article constructs a picture, a distorted one, of the 'West Side' through racialized and classed signifiers.

In both of these examples, and in many other articles, the West Side has been underpinned by a discourse that repeatedly represents the inhabitants as well as the space as criminal, deficient and foreign. The persistence of and continuity in the meanings of the construct suggest that it has attained the status of knowledge. An unquestionable truth has settled over the construct as the media and city residents have repeated it with the same cluster of signifiers and have coordinated programs and resources to "develop" or "help" the West Side.

Meanwhile, the East Side construct has had minimal presence in the media. Historically, it emerges in the media coupled to language that provides a pastoral image of property that is for sale on the east side of the city. For example, one advertisement in a 1907 local newspaper exemplifies the general pattern of use of the East Side term when it indicates, "The owner will sell direct one of the most beautiful homes in the east side. On the only macadamized street in east side of city" (The Salt Lake Evening Telegram, 1907). The dominance of white residents in this area has never been scrutinized by residents in media venues, as the alleged pervasiveness of Spanish speakers has been on the other side of the city. This pattern of invisibility in the media is consistent for most of the twentieth century. By 2000, the local media has given the local meanings around the East Side construct more thought as discussions arise in television and newspaper coverage regarding the various dimensions (i.e., geographical, racial, class, religious) of the East Side and West Side division. Specifically, conversations center around the assumptions residents hold about these spaces and their inhabitants. This coverage generally finds that people's imaginary of each section of town follows the following logic, "Looking for espresso stands? Sports utility vehicles? Large houses in leafy suburbs? Head East. In search of fast-food joints? Pickup trucks? Mobile homes? Taco stands? Go West" (Baird, 2000).

The Convergence of Discourse, Material Relations, and Practices

The historical construction of the East Side and West Side space is an effect of the simultaneous interaction between the organization of the material realm, the social meanings of this space and the practices of city residents. All three dimensions have converged to produce the social ecology of Salt Valley City as differentiated people and space. The material organization of these different spaces (i.e. housing; zoning of city lots; industrial buildings; green, leafy neighborhoods) needs to be seen in relationship to the deployment of the meanings about these spaces and the inhabitants who reside there. The temporal heuristic that we align ourselves with here is one of simultaneous activity and interaction. Put differently, the socio-historical organization of housing and employment is underpinned by a local knowledge, or discourse, that denotes and justifies who belongs where, or who is capable of accomplishing particular tasks (i.e., mental vs. labor).

The framing of this history, we readily admit, has a slightly functionalist emphasis to it; that is, the narrative suggests an effective, purposeful incorporation of these cultural codes into the vocabularies and practices of city residents. There has been, however, conflict and disputes over the division of the city space and people, as well as over the representations of those who live on the western side of the city as deficit, dirty and criminal. These conflicts, however, have pertained to educational issues primarily, specifically the redrawing of school boundaries as a remedy to educational segregation and as high schools have been closed due to a diminishing student population (Kantor, 2004). City residents have engaged in very little contestation over politicians' usage of the constructs West Side or East Side over the twentieth century, or of the consolidation of working class people of color on the West Side of the city or whites on the East. Instead, the ordering of space as well as the terms employed to define it has retained a naturalness among city residents and the media.

CHAPTER 4

EAST SIDE/WEST SIDE:
THE SPATIAL PRODUCTION OF DIFFERENTIATED STUDENTS AND SPACES

In talking to principals or teachers from either the western or eastern side of Salt Valley City about their school, their students or their work, you quickly get a sense that there's something different between their school and students and others elsewhere in the city. This difference is communicated in subtle terms like "Here, in West Side schools we focus on" or "Up here, our students are." For the most, these spatial markers of the West Side or East Side were rarely defined, but employed in ways that assumed that their meanings were known to all. Occasionally, the opposing pole of the comparison–either the East Side, West Side or down there–was made transparent in conversations, and the meanings of each construct were also defined so that listeners realized that these spatial codes denoted meanings about race and class. In other discussions, educators deployed the spatial codes without the list of propositions but used them in a way that indexed, or indirectly referred to, these meanings. These spatial markers resembled greatly the historical meanings of the West Side and East Side that have been deployed locally by city politicians and its media. They had, however, a slight nuance to them about intellectual ability and needs that differentiated them from what was found in other city conversations.

In this chapter, we turn our attention to the production of these spatial codes within the city's schools. We examine how Salt Valley District's teachers and principals participated in the social production of the East Side and West Side student, school and space. The argument that we develop in this chapter is that schools do not solely inherit, or are victim to, local discourses but participate actively in the production of a knowledge of these students, schools and spaces. Our use of the term "production" implies that educators engage in acts of discursive construction and material coordination to create a specific institutional knowledge of the West Side and East Side. This production involves the local knowledge that we identified in the previous chapter as well as other national discourses that are specific to educational institutions. We show how this knowledge retained many elements of the citywide discourse, particularly the racial and classed elements, yet also had other historical educational strands, such as deficit and at-risk educational discourses, that circulate in national educational policy.

Furthermore, we argue that while educators co-produced these racial and class denoting discourses, they also employed them in ways that hid the overtones of racial and class difference. These spatial codes were employed in ways that seemed, on the surface, genteel and innocent. These uses, however, had a great deal of potency in coordinating and legitimating differential educational programs and knowledge, as well as in the citywide discourses of particular populations and spaces. The pervasiveness of this knowledge within Salt Valley's schools contributed to the re-segregation and segmentation of city space by adding one more institutional relation within the landscape of the city that functioned from and produced these meanings of these spaces and people that circulated citywide. Lastly, we argue that the process of producing this knowledge was not one solely involving discourse. We describe how educators organized different material technologies such as funding apparatuses, curricular materials and organizational structures in a way that enmeshed and naturalized these representations so that they had a material dimension.

We Are a West Side School with West Side Students

Most educators from the western side of the city did not hesitate in stating, "We are West Side schools teaching West Side students." For educators from this part of the city, the West Side signifier had a great deal of social and pedagogical significance in speaking about their students, their mission as teachers and how they are different from other schools in the city, and about place. The knowledge of the West Side student is a durable assemblage of socially constructed propositions about the racial and class identities of students and their families that provided educators with a knowledge of the alleged aspirations and life choices of these subjects. Educators produced and employed this knowledge to help them make sense of and bring order to the realm of student and school identity, as well as enable them to act within institutions where a firm sense of subject and place is necessary.

There were many instances when educators from the West Side of the city made transparent the institutional meanings of the West Side school, student and space. This discourse was ever present when educators began to discuss who their students were and what they needed educationally. The West Side construct was explicitly coupled to signifiers such as "the poor," "the ethnic," "the non-English speaking," "the educationally uninterested" and "the at-risk" to define an ontology (i.e., concept of being) of the West Side subject and space. These terms were repeatedly coupled together in such a way that they had a deficit connotation, or a meaning of students and families as intellectually lacking, morally suspect and socially inferior (Valencia, 1997). For example, note how the terms "poor," "immigrants," and legal status were brought together by this white, female teacher to present a common meaning of West Side students as criminal and outside of a rarely stated norm.

> Interviewer: So, who are your students?
> White Female Teacher: Well here, and at other West Side schools in the district, they come from a poor family. Immigrants, usually. It's common at our school, that they're not here legally. Their parents are in and out of jobs. They have a high mobility rate. (See Appendix for Transcription Conventions)

Students and families from this part of the city were repeatedly represented in these terms of the impoverished and the socially marginal. Terms that denoted lower socio-economic class, as in the reference to parents who are "in and out of jobs," as well as race and ethnicity, the use of "immigrants," were consistently linked to the term West Side. Even in instances where factual, demographic information was elicited, the West Side signifier retained its deficit logic. Educators presented this information in a linguistic structure, or grammar (Gee, 1999), where students and families from this part were deemed economically and socially unstable. As an example,

> I: How is life here at Hoover Elementary (a school who identifies, and is identified, as being West Side) as compared to, let's say, Wilson (a school who identifies, and is identified, as an East Side school)?
> White Male Elementary Principal (E.P.): I'd say the demographics. The single parents, the language issues, now the refugee issue is coming. When I first came here, there were no non-English speaking students. The poverty rate was like twenty percent, and the minority rate was like fifteen percent. And now the poverty rate is up ninety-four percent at most West Side schools. Then the other factor was that we only have about twenty-five percent of the school is currently Anglo. Less than that are stable.

The discourse employed here to describe the demographics coupled all of the central linguistic units, the impoverished, the non-English speaker, and the non-white. This principal's concluding point that "less than that are stable" puts an evaluative spin on this representation so that stability was premised on ontological characteristics, all attributes that the new population allegedly do not possess.

West Side Educators

The ontology of the West Side teacher was also produced in this process. Similar to the discourses of the West Side student, the identity of teachers as "West Side teachers" as well as the nature and scope of their work was entangled in the institutional knowledge of the West Side. The construction of student and family ontology as one of having few intellectual or social assets and needing to be saved from themselves underpinned educators' concept of educating. This shared discourse of educational practice integrated elements of a social work discourse to it, one where the emphasis was on educators changing students' and families' life situations through the modification of personal behaviors, as well as the institutional management and treatment of the whole child. The entanglement of this discourse of educating and that of the West Side student was evident as teachers talked about their daily activities and the uniqueness of their work. There was a shared sense that the work of a "West Side teacher" and, ultimately, "West Side school" was different than others in the city.

These differences between schools, students and educators' work were articulated by a group of teachers as they discussed the design and mission of their school in relation to another school in another part of the city. The following conversation demonstrates how the spatial knowledge of West Side students and families merges with that of teachers' mission in a way so that they are consonant with each other.

> White Female Teacher 1: I remember when we were designing our school, we went on a field trip down to, was it Pheasant Run [School]? (Turning to the other teachers in the room)
> White Female Teacher 2: Uh huh.
> White Female Teacher 1: After we left we kept saying, "What was funny or odd?" We couldn't quite figure out what was wrong with that school and we got about half way home and somebody said, "There were 19 blonde kids in that class." And we were like, "Oh, *that* was the problem!" You know because for us West Side teachers it's just everyday when you see a parent in the hall and you say a few words and then you try your broken Spanish on them and they try their broken English on you.

This reference to the racial difference between their students and those of Pheasant Run, specifically their pointing to the "oddness" of "19 blond kids," shows how their conception of student body and work were intertwined. The

West Side student body is positioned in this conversation by stating what it is not, white and English speaking. After locating the difference in contexts through racial markers, teachers then used this difference to contrast themselves and their work from Pheasant Run teachers. They deduced that the work of Pheasant Run teachers was not like theirs, one of negotiating and learning new languages and teaching students and families who supposedly had few intellectual skills.

This point of difference around the relationship between socially constructed student ontology and educational mission is an important one because it is where educators produced and instantiated a particular institutional knowledge of the West Side teacher and student. They coupled together different discourses–elements of a social work, the deficit and the local spatial West Side/East Side discourse–to produce a spatially specific, institutional knowledge that gave institutional meaning to the West Side student and teacher. To elaborate on this point, another example from the data might help us to illustrate the integration and overlap of these different discourses to construct an institutionally specific knowledge of the West Side student and teacher. What is important in the following conversation is how the discourse of the whole child, the altering of behaviors through programs, and teachers' educational practices are integrated to speak to the uniqueness of teaching at this "West Side" school.

> Interviewer: So what defines teaching here at Roosevelt? [a school whose teachers self defined as West Side]
> White Female Teacher 1: We have a lot of challenges. We have parents who because they speak a different language or, perhaps, they never went beyond sixth or seventh grade have come to my classroom and have asked me to teach them. This may be a third or a second grade child, and the parents have asked me to teach them so that they can help their child₁
> White Female Teacher 2: [Because they don't have the intellectual skills to assist their child outside of the classroom, whereas in other schools most kids can go home and ask mom, dad, or older brother.
> White Female Teacher 1: They're unable to get more help outside of the school so we've incorporated programs that try to help the parents, train the parents, give them support so that they can help their child at home.

The range of tasks and programs that these teachers and others from this part of the city defined as their work encompassed not just students but also educating students' parents. This holistic approach to their work was what these teachers saw as differentiating their mode of educating, their students and their space from other teachers. We can also use this latter conversation as a rejoinder to the earlier remark made by the other group of teachers about the "oddness" of Pheasant Run school. The oddness centers, we might venture, around the difference in mission, self and student.

Indexing a Knowledge of the West Side

While the instances in which educators spelled out the meanings of the West Side student and teacher were many, there were just as many other occasions when the West Side construct was deployed in an indexical manner, or one in which the propositions underpinning it were not explicitly articulated but understood between speakers as an underlying, common and consensually agreed upon local knowledge (Bakhtin, 1986). Educators' indexical use of these constructs is illuminating because it demonstrates the power and pervasiveness of these constructs as a local school knowledge. It was in educators' professional discussions about their practice, students and space that they used the indexical, shorthand form. This usage permitted educators to name and order the world of schools, classrooms and the city in the racialized and classed discourse while, at the same time, obscuring these meanings from public view. It was what might be perceived as a genteel form, or code, of locating the knowledge of racial and class distinctions without ever actually articulating them. Educators' usage of and activities around these codes facilitated their participation in the division and re-segregation of city relations by enacting a West Side/East Side binary that was specific to educational institutions. Furthermore, these practices brought a degree of naturalness to these constructs within Salt Valley City Schools such that educators did not have to question the meanings and legitimacy of this knowledge, due in part to the historical patterns of usage within the broader city.

The indexical use of the West Side construct was employed, for the most, in juxtaposition to the East Side signifier. Educators constructed and instantiated a binary where each was understood as an opposite in terms of their racial and classed meanings. While distinctions in race and class were subtly delineated through this juxtaposition, the binary also functioned to denote distinct spaces of the city. The way that the indexical use performed this dual function was evident in "West Side" educators' discussions of their school mission and their practice. Note in the following conversation between a group of teachers and one of the authors how a binary was constructed between West Side and East Side so that class differences were initially delineated without explicitly spelling them out. It is only after a few seconds of silence between the interviewer and the teachers where the propositions underpinning each were delineated.

> White Elementary Teacher 1: As a faculty we realize that our West Side parents don't have the opportunities that the East Side parents have. / /₁
> Interviewer: ⌊ / /
> White Elementary Teacher 2: So, we're advocating for parents. We're going to teach you how you can read with your child. We're going to give you the things that you can't afford, and the skills that you need. We're going to give you the E.S.L. [English as a Second Language] classes to help further your English. We're going to give you those references to those, uh, support kind of issues, healthcare, clothing.

The typical stream of signifiers that explicitly defined West Side students and families (i.e., poor, non-English speaking, intellectually lacking) were not initially spelled out by the first teacher in this instantiation. Instead, the first teacher provided a point of contrast that alluded to understood differences in economic situations, or opportunities, and intellectual and linguistic skills between East Side and West Side subjects. The teachers, however, seemed to interpret the pause in the conversation as a break down, or gap, in the shared knowledge between discussants of these differences. What followed was the typical list of knowledge propositions about these subjects.

In other conversations with teachers, discussions ensued using the indexical form without ever spelling out the implied meanings. In many of these, a distinct space was also clearly marked out. That is, educators instantiated the concept of a geographically bound and established place. The following representation demonstrates a typical conversation enacted by teachers that self-defined as West Side in which they, first, indexed differences in ways that peers seemed to understand and, second, marked out a space whose boundaries seemed clearly delineated.

> White Elementary Teacher 1: When we did the institute this summer, one of the schools that we went with to talk about [curricular and pedagogical] problems and what we were doing was Alta [a school who is identified as, and who self identifies as, an East Side school]. And not in a million years would we have ever thought we could have something to discuss with their teachers, just because it's₁
> White Elementary Teacher 2: ⌈it's so different from east to west.
> White Elementary Teacher 3: Yeah.

The terms of this "difference" were never spelled out in this discussion, or many others similar to this one. Yet, its meanings were never ambiguous to the other educators. The production of meaning in all of these conversations was fluid and uninterrupted. The manner and consistency in which these constructs were explicitly defined in other institutional and citywide conversations facilitated moments like these where the indexical form had a clarity and naturalness that made sense to all.

The same was true in demarcating the space of the East Side and West Side. Educators had a clear sense of the geography of the city. As the conversation above shows, there is, in the minds of educators, a clear East and West Side, and clear differences between them. The objects of this geography, though, were other schools, teachers and students. We never encountered a debate or disagreement amongst these educators over the designation of a school as a West Side or East Side school, or whether it was actually on the East Side or West Side of the city. The truth telling power of the construct in these conversations suggested that this knowledge had reached a level of institutional saliency where it needed no explanation.

We Are East Side Up Here

The designation East Side served a similar function as that of West Side in schools that self-identified, and were identified by others, as "East Side" schools. Like "West Side" schools, there were instances when educators spelled out the list of propositions tied to this construct, and others where it was used in the indexical form. The use, however, was not as widely employed as its counterpart, West Side. Similar to its public appearance in the city's media or its uses by local politicians, the East Side construct had a degree of illusiveness, or invisibility, within elementary schools that educators identified as East Side. Instead, these educators employed spatial synonyms of "up here" and "down there" to designate an ontology of student and teacher as well as a concept of space.

The meanings that educators coupled to the East Side were polar opposites to those articulated to describe the West Side student, teacher and school. What educators produced and instantiated was an institutional knowledge of the East Side, or the up here, as a "well prepared," "intellectually-abled," and "educationally invested" student and family. They discursively constructed a spatial subject of student, teacher and school that linked these propositions to produce a knowledge of this subject as well as locate it geographically. For example, in the instances when educators explicitly deployed the East Side signifier to define an ontology of the East

Side subject, these propositions were coupled together to construct individuals as "successful" students and "supportive" and "astute" families. This was evident as educators began to describe

> Interviewer: A common theme at other schools was matching content to students' backgrounds in order to facilitate success. Is this important here?
> Female Elementary Teacher 1: I think particularly at East Side schools, it's [matching content to students' experiential base] not really asked or thought about very much because kids are fairly successful no matter what you teach them. They come ready to learn. They come with great genes, you know.
> Female Elementary Teacher 2: So, as far as achievement, we're lucky. We have a lot of kids who come to school here with a decent night's sleep and either really clean, or pretty clean, clothes on their backs. There's that value on education, they care about school.

The propositions comprising this knowledge of East Side students as "fairly successful no matter what," having "great genes," and "valu[ing] education" presented listeners with a shared knowledge of an ideal student. Conversations between educators from these schools proceeded over and over that suggested that there was consensus that these propositions were true. Like the conversation represented above, this knowledge was employed in a seamless fashion, or a feeling and appearance of a natural and a-temporal state.

Unlike the racial motifs of the West Side, the knowledge of the East Side student consistently presented a student that was raceless. In the preceding quote, the reference to "great genes" may refer to a racial lineage, but its presence and meaning is somewhat ambiguous. The socio-economic class markers of the East Side student were, for the most, more prominent than the racial ones. Educators from these schools employed subtle references that defined specific markings of social class. In the conversation represented above, this was carried out through the reference to "clean clothes" and "decent night's sleep." In others, references to travel and endless parental involvement identified how economic privilege translated into parents' flexibility in organizing their time.

These linguistic markers to a raceless yet economically privileged student and family were particularly poignant as references to a specific space, the East Side, were stated. While the instances in which the East Side was specifically named were limited, the times in which it was employed it sought to make a spatial distinction between East Side and typically an unnamed space that was the West Side. This delineation and juxtaposition became clearer as we followed the production and use of the spatial synonyms of the "up here" and "down there" by these educators.

Up Here, Not Down There

Educators from the East Side of the city defined a discursive spatial and ontological divide by discussing differences between an "up here" and "down there." These terms functioned synonymously as the East Side/West Side constructs in that they named particular ontological traits and spatial relations of the city's students and schools. They consistently denoted difference along the line of the East Side/West Side binary without specifically naming the East Side. These terms functioned in the indexical manner that was evident in schools on the western side of the city. However, this use typically included the usual list of propositions about the West Side and indexed the meanings tied to the East Side construct. Put differently, educators rendered the East Side construct invisible in their talk, as well as juxtaposed the list of propositions that cohered as the knowledge of the East Side and the West Side.

For example, the manner in which these educators employed the term "up here" was repeatedly contrasted to ontological signifiers such as immigrant, politically ignorant, and spatio-ontological terms such as inner city. Note how this principal envisioned parents' participation based on these spatio-ontological discourses.

> Male Elementary Principal: Parents are going to want to have a lot of input into sex education here. Whereas in a culture or in a West Side school where you've got more of an immigrant population, that may be the last thing in the back of their minds, simply because they're trying to figure out how to survive. So up here I'm going to be a little more attentive to parent input than I might have to be down there in an inner city school. The constraints up here I think are more political in nature. I don't have stupid parents. And by stupid or uneducated or anything like that, not that the parents down there are, but these are savvy parents.

The distinctions between "up here" and "down there" were clearly distinguished in a binary fashion in this conversation. The spatial marker "up here" was juxtaposed to the signifiers West Side and inner city that geographically located schools on the eastern side of the city as lying somewhere else other than the inner city. Yet, this difference was not solely geographical. This distinction suggested a difference at the level of ontology. Terms such as "cultural," "immigrant" and "naive" were used repeatedly as counterpoints to define an inferred, undefined entity, or the white, East Side "savvy parent." In practice, the reference to the inner city and those down there pointed to a racial and class subject that needed little explanation. This conversation does not stray too far from the local newspaper articles that juxtaposed the space of the demi-monde or of the junk collecting West Side and the green lawned, cappuccino set that resides on the East Side.

A theme that was also central in statements such as the one above is the difference in educational tasks, or work, between the educators in these schools and those defined as West Side, a point of conversation also prevalent in schools that self-defined as West Side. A common topic found in these conversations was that the mission of these schools was very different from those "down there." The principal's statement above articulates this difference in referring to the level of attentiveness that he has to devote to his parents, as opposed to what he assumes for principals who work with immigrant, inner-city schools. In other discussions with educators from these schools this was made more explicit as they defined their work as not social work and their students as having few social problems. What follows are representations of two different conversations with one group of teachers and one principal from two different schools where these representations were instantiated:

> Interviewer: So what do you think the purpose of schools should be?
> Female Elementary Teacher: Well I think it should be to educate children, not to solve the social ills of families and kids necessarily. I think when we expand our mission that broadly, we lose that focus on education and we can spend our whole time being social workers. ...I think when we try to do that, we really lose our primary purpose and then we really have no reason for being if we're not educating children well.

Lastly,

> Interviewer: Schools such as Loma, Garfield, and Adams [schools that are identified and self-identified as West Side schools] emphasized matching students and families to social services to help their students. Is that the case here?
> Female Elementary Principal: Up here it's kind of a stigma for the child. And where they, down there on the West Side, are only concerned with social kinds of issues, here its kind of a flip-flop. Academics come first.

The distinctions that these educators constructed about their educational mission and practice centered around student identity and place. However, these differences were predicated on illusive attributes that had more to do with what these students were not–West Side–than what they were. The use of the construct "up here" is an important entity in these conversations because it indexed the list of propositions about East Side students and families that were not stated publicly, for the most. This spatio-ontological marker also appeared to bring order to the educational mission and activities of these educators, one that was narrowly defined as educating the mind. Their sense of appropriate practices and programs was hinged, in part, on the distinction and division between who is and what is in place "down there" on the West Side, and what it means economically, racially, and socially to live "up here" on the foothills. In other words, educators' concept of what is educationally fitting for students and families up on the East Side is caught up in the social knowledge of different spaces and spatial subjects that are named the West Side/East Side.

Spatialized and Spatializing Technologies of East Side/West Side

The picture that we have presented thus far in this chapter is one of the discursive practices that educators have produced and enacted to construct West Side and East Side students, teachers and schools. This production of spatial subjects and space, however, also involved the interplay of material technologies in further spatializing, or re-instantiating a spatial dimension through spatial relations (Shields, 1997), already spatialized practices and knowledge. Within the broader city, socio-historical technologies such as local newspapers, racial covenants built into bank's lending notes, housing market prices, the construction of business offices in the downtown, and the railroad lines that cut across the city all functioned to spatialize, segment and segregate the city into a West Side and an East Side. Many of these technologies also worked to propagate this knowledge of populations and space. Schools, too, participated in this spatialization. Schools had institutionally specific technologies that were coordinated for them and by them that spatialized subjects and worked in conjunction with these other citywide technologies to spatialize the city.

The institutional technologies that schools employed included apparatuses such as federal and state funding mechanisms and the elements of a recently initiated district-wide reform involving curriculum re-organization and inter-school clusters, or groupings. The reform, as practices and the coordination of material objects and bodies, was the most recent catalyst in sustaining this spatial knowledge. The elements of the reform were efficiently and seamlessly aligned and connected to pre-existing school technologies that helped to re-produce and instantiate the space and knowledge of the East Side/West Side. They were both a spatialized and spatializing technology in producing these distinctions. That is, the reform was initiated within the existing logic of the West Side/East Side binary (the spatilized quality) and operated to organize other practices and technologies so that they corresponded to this knowledge (the spatializing element).

Prior to discussing the reform and how it functioned to produce and reproduce social meanings and relations, we need to highlight a few of the district-wide technologies that preceded the reform. These, too, had spatial and spatializing qualities that shaped how the reform was ultimately aligned. The most prominent of these were federal and state funding. The distribution of federal and state monies within the district worked to define schools and students as having particular attributes and also consolidated spatially these fiscal technologies, which were converted to deficit oriented programs and services, within schools that were located on the West Side of the city.

To begin with, the language for determining eligibility of both state and federal monies foregrounded the racial and classed attributes of students that were discursively presented as "at risk" determiners. For example, the state's Highly Impacted Schools funding was under the umbrella of the state's "Youth At-Risk Programs." Alongside the structural organization of these funds under "at-risk" programs, the state deployed a discourse in the eligibility criteria that represented recipients as disadvantaged, criminal, and morally questionable. This was explicit in the language of whom the program was targeting: "(a) youth in custody; (b) adolescent pregnancy prevention; (c) homeless and disadvantaged minority students; (d) mathematics, engineering, and science achievement programs; (e) gang prevention and intervention" (Minimal School Program Act, p. 14). With the exception of the reference to math and science achievement programs, the rest of this list has an ominous ring of individuals on the edge of society and in need of social rehabilitation. The listing of "disadvantaged minority students" alongside the signifiers "youth in custody," "gangs" and "adolescent pregnancy" renders ethnicity and poverty as being on par with criminal and sexual behavior.

This discourse overlapped with federal funding technologies so that their integration was unfettered by contradictory frameworks. Federally funded free and reduced lunch programs, as well as the monies from Title I of the federal No Child Left Behind Act (NCLB), also employed the discourse of at-risk. The propositions that federal and state technologies shared were that at-risk status could be determined through attributes of racial identity, cultural practices (i.e., language) and social class. Note the overlap in the language of the federal Title I - Improving the Academic Achievement of the Disadvantaged (2001) policy to the list of signifiers employed above in the state Highly Impacted Schools policy:

> The purpose of this title is to ensure that all children have a fair, equal, and significant opportunity to obtain a high quality education ...by—(2) meeting the educational needs of low-achieving children in our Nation's high poverty schools, limited English proficient children, migratory children, children with disabilities, Indian children, neglected or delinquent children, and young children in need of reading assistance. (The National Clearinghouse for Bilingual Education, Title I, p. 17)

While the language seems merely descriptive, the fact that this is found in a document about the "disadvantaged" cannot be lost. It couples together, similar to the state policy, terms that place children who are poor and of color in a de facto state of at risk and disadvantaged. Other sections of the federal policy employed language that explicitly matched the state's policy, such as the Authorization of Appropriations section that stated its purpose is the, "(d) Prevention and Intervention Programs for Youth Who Are Neglected, Delinquent, or At Risk" (The National Clearinghouse for Bilingual Education, Title I, p. 18). While there are, indeed, limitations within school spaces when students do not speak English fluently or may not have financial resources, we question, though, the logic that this discourse advances that equates race, language and social class as inherent disadvantages or attributes of at-risk. Such associations render institutions and institutional practices as unproblematic and, instead, place institutional shortfalls on the shoulders of students (see, for example, Gitlin, Buendía, Crosland, Doumbia, 2003; Olsen, 1997; Valenzuela, 1999). The point that we want to underscore here, however, is that the state and federal financial technologies were underpinned by a similar discourse that rendered its recipients as at-risk.

While these funding technologies (as programs and personnel) constructed an at-risk and disadvantaged subject, the spatial consolidation of these material resources within schools on the western edge of the city is equally important in producing a spatial distinction within schools. As schools translated state and federal funding technologies into programs and people (i.e., after school gang prevention programs, drug and alcohol resistance education, additional counselors and teacher assistants) for students inscribed as at-risk and disadvantaged, these programs became spatialized technologies due to their placement within city schools on the West Side of the city. The effect was a material instantiation of the conceptual division in the district's schools where demarcations of the disadvantaged and, implicitly, advantaged were made clearly identifiable. In other words, the division between East Side and West Side schools and students was further buttressed so that the difference was not solely conceptual, but so that it also had real, material technologies that corresponded to this knowledge. The alignment of "words and things" (Foucault, 1972) confirmed for educators that the distinctions between these schools and students were indeed authentic.

The Spatialized and Spatializing Reform

As the coordination and spatial consolidation of fiscal and programmatic technologies institutionalized the historical spatial distinctions that existed within the city, these technologies also worked, over time, as spatializing elements as other educational curricula and innovations were adopted in schools. Educators adoption and incorporation of new educational curricula, programs and practices were discursively and structurally aligned and integrated to work with the pre-existing technologies so that they, too, had a geographical continuity that reflected the logic of the East Side and West Side.

The most recent example of this spatialization was a reform initiative within the district's elementary schools that sought to move educators towards better advocacy for their low-achieving students, encourage adoptions of school literacy programs that were based on data, and foster more efficient inter-school coordination, to name its central goals. The district office, through the assistance of a national foundation, made small amounts of funding available for these activities as each school constructed a school plan to enact practices around these goals. The hub of most of the reform's activity centered around the adoptions of new literacy programs. Schools opted for four literacy series, all varying in price as well as emphasis. The most expensive programs were series such as Success For All (SFA) and the California Early Literacy/Extended Literacy Learning (CEL/xLL). These two encompassed rigidly scripted phonics instruction, an extensive array of instructional materials (e.g., basal readers, workbooks, DVDs) and directed and continuous coaching and assessment for teachers and principals. The other two were less a formal series and represented more of a balanced literature model or framework (i.e., open-ended and varied phonics instruction and authentic literature readings and resources). The elements of these latter programs included a compilation of literature and a cadre of recommended literacy instructional practices. More specifically, the third option included a list of selected texts from Scholastic Basal Adoptions and Houghton Mifflin, and the last one had no designated publishing house or set series and was the most flexible, or least prescriptive, for teachers. It was termed by teachers as Learning For All (LFA).

The selection and coordination of literacy programs is where the integration of pre-existing and new technologies was most evident. Moreover, it was also through these processes in which the new educational technologies were spatialized. First, the integration was facilitated by the ability of schools on the West Side of the city to combine their federal Title I and state Highly Impacted School funds to purchase the expensive phonics driven, and remedial oriented, literacy programs. These schools had the financial resources to make these types of purchases, unlike schools on the eastern side of the city that did not qualify for federal or state funds such as these. Principals from these schools repeatedly described how they integrated the two funds so that they worked together (discursively and materially) to meet the goals of advocacy and the adoption of new literacy programs.

> Male Principal: Well, federal Title I monies are targeted at our at-risk students, whereas, our reform grant [monies] was to be allotted for low performing students. The two dove tailed nicely so that we could combine them to buy programs that we would have never been able to otherwise.

The discourses delineating the purposes of these funding technologies, as targeting the disadvantaged or at-risk, linked and entangled the new instructional technologies with pre-existing federal and state funds. Secondly, the educators in "West Side" schools with these monies summoned and aligned themselves with the discourse of "at risk" and the "disadvantaged" to talk about their students and their school. With the convergence of these spatial relations, educators from these schools surveyed the different literacy programs and deemed the remedial emphasis of the heavily phonics driven programs as "fitting" the profile of their students. Educators' conversion of fiscal technologies into instructional ones retained the discourse of the disadvantaged. The temporal (historical) gap in the placement of these technologies (i.e., funds and programs) within schools was reconciled as educators' practices facilitated the enmeshment of these different technologies.

This integration of these technologies within particular schools and not others also buttressed the historical spatial distinctions so that the new literacy technologies and practices associated with them were spatialized. As we have described, the federal and state monies functioned as spatializing elements that spurred, in part, the spatial consolidation of the expensive and remedial literacy programs within schools that were identified and self-identified as West Side. The assemblage of resources that were meant to help was employed in a fashion that reproduced the division. Only two schools in this block opted for the Scholastic/Houghton Mifflin series. Meanwhile, schools that identified as East Side chose the more flexibly oriented Learning For All model, under the auspices that, first, they did not have the money for the expensive all inclusive programs and, second, these did not fit the needs or profile of their students.

This process of spatialization of instructional technologies programs was not solely a question of finances. The knowledge of the East Side and West Side also came into play as educators created and enacted educational structures and professional practices around other elements of the reform, specifically the inter-school collaboration, or what the authors of the reform termed "clustering for cohesion." Once schools across the district made their literacy programs adoptions, the next activity that educators engaged in was identifying other schools that were similar to them so that they could collaborate in the professional development around these programs. These clusters, or groupings, took on a spatialized quality, however. The adoption of expensive, phonics based programs by schools on the West Side of the city propelled educators in these schools to forge formal relationships with other "West Side" schools in order to share the costs of training. The same held true with schools that self-identified as East Side, due to their lack of resources as well as a shared knowledge of self and students as East Side teachers and students. The effect of these activities was East Side clusters and West Side clusters.

The importance of these clusters in solidifying the knowledge and structural arrangements of the East Side/West Side division lies not only in the consolidation of particular programs but also in the practices that educators coordinated around the technology of clusters. These involved practices of sharing information that validated and assured educators that they and their students were, ontologically and spatially, who and what they thought they were, either West Side or East Side. The practice of talking about an "our" and a "we" as well as the needs that are inherent to this collective provided educators with a sense of a bounded place and a firm sense of identity. The imagined community (Anderson, 2000) of West Side and East Side practitioners became real through interaction.

As an example of how this manifested, notice in the following quotation how this group of educators in schools that self-identified as West Side were joined in clusters that helped them to envision themselves as West Side schools with West Side students, as well as enabled them to practice this spatialized identity:

> Elementary Principal: Clustering for cohesion with respect to Adams, Wasatch and Smith, who are all SFA schools, we've pretty much been you know, working in this together for the last three years. It has brought our faculty together for collective training. It gives teachers an opportunity to share among themselves and each other from other schools, talk about what's happening, what they're experiencing. We've been able to work on strategies that we can all share.

Similar sentiments were shared by teachers from the eastern side of the city who created clusters based on the Learning For All model. The ability of educators to articulate shared strategies that are applicable to all necessitates that the teachers from these schools agree that they have many similarities in their student populations. There must be a consensus that there is, indeed, a "we." Sharing, in itself, involves an agreement that your context is similar to mine. To buttress this point, here is one more statement that encapsulated how the majority of the schools in clusters rationalized the groupings based on a belief of similar students and space.

> EP: Well we clustered based on the direction that we're going with our literacy plan. Because that involved a lot of professional development. We're in the same environments anyway.

A spatialized identity of teachers was practiced among objects such as literacy elements and a shared concept of place. Space, objects and practices functioned to produce a collective identity denoted as "we."

The literacy programs and the literacy clusters that were components of the reform exemplified how new technologies interfaced with each other and were spatialized by pre-existing ones. These technologies took on spatialized and spatializing qualities. They were coordinated, in other words, by other pre-existing technologies to fit within the knowledge of the spatial distinctions of the West Side/East Side and became, ultimately, apparatuses that shaped how new technologies functioned within the spaces of schools. The institutional practices of educators were crucial to their integration. Practices such as educators convening monthly to converse and share instructional materials and pedagogical strategies around the literacy programs and models, as well as their spending of federal and state funds (or lack thereof) to do this integrated these elements so that educators and schools experienced a seamlessness in these overlapping technologies. In paraphrasing Pierre Bourdieu (1990), educators' practices "objectively harmonized without any calculation or conscious reference to a norm and mutually adjusted in the absence of any direct interaction or, *a fortiori*, explicit co-ordination" (p. 59) the field of knowledge and relations to work within the existing historical knowledge of the East Side/West Side.

Summary

This chapter has sought to show how the East Side and West Side constructs are an institutional knowledge that is also produced by educators within schools. Educators employed these broader socio-historical constructs and coupled educational discourses to them that constructed West Side students as deficit and East Side students as an invisible norm and superior student. Educators also employed this knowledge to define their concept of mission and work. Both groups of educators engaged in educational practices that were consonant with the knowledge produced about each respective group of students. They also coordinated a range of material technologies that functioned within the spatial logic of this knowledge and that worked in spatializing other, new, practices and technologies.

This chapter has presented a degree of tidiness that is not necessarily the case for the district as a whole. The binary of the East Side and West Side has a third element to it that has started to emerge within school discussions in the form of the construct Central City. The following chapter examines this other knowledge and space, and explains how this construct has hybridized the knowledge of the East Side and West Side to become something different.

CHAPTER 5

THE CENTRAL CITY SCHOOLS:
THE AMBIGUITIES OF THE BORDERLANDS

Although the spaces defined or identified as East Side and West Side have developed over time to be fairly defined and bounded in the city's imaginary, immigration and a recent (e.g., 10 years) rapid increase in numbers of people of color has created some fluidity within the West Side especially. A pattern has formed by which immigrants move into existing West Side neighborhoods, establish themselves economically, and then move to other parts of the Valley. Given the economic landscape, including housing prices, the parts of the Valley available for upwardly mobile people of color lie close to but east of the freeway and railroad yards. As such, an area of increasing ethnic/racial, linguistic, and socioeconomic diversity that is expanding from west to east across the Salt Lake Valley can be seen as creating a spatial border that is shifting over time. Parts of the East Side are now a destination for immigrants both from afar (for example, international students attending local universities, and their families) and from the West Side. As a result, schools as well as neighborhoods are experiencing change as spaces that have historically been homogeneous white and middle class are becoming demographically heterogeneous (the District experienced an average 8% yearly increase in students of color between 1997 and 2003, and by 2004, white students made up 49% of the total student population).

Importantly, what is changing is the demographic make-up of this part of the Valley, but not the built environment. Very little of the physical space has changed over time, which may help explain why the Central City construct has not been invoked in the broader discourses of the city, including governmental institutions and the media. Schools, we will show, were actively constructing this dynamic Central City space, particularly their students, as new and different. As such, educators were engaged in spatializing the area through the practices, technologies and knowledge they adopted in response to increasing numbers of children and families of color entering their doors. They were also working to redefine themselves as educators and their schools in relation to what had been an East Side space.

A collection of eight schools caught our attention in the process of data analysis initially because they did not claim an East Side or a West Side label. The result was a discursive ambiguity that characterized their talk, as educators did not explicitly claim a label and rarely used the existing binary to identify themselves and their schools. As we explored this interesting discourse, we looked to see what relationships might tie the schools together. What piqued our interest in critically examining the cultural geography of the Valley and its schools was the fact that the 8 schools all lie physically along that corridor over which the eastward-moving line of increasing diversity is crossing most recently. Situated between the flatter, more crowded clines of downtown and the steeper, more spacious foothills, these schools have demographic profiles similar to West Side schools; however, the changes in their student populations and surrounding communities have happened more recently than schools who are physically on the west of the downtown area and who explicitly claim West Side as an identifying signifier.

Self-referents in talk and in school documents sometimes used the term "Central City," pointing to an emerging construct in which the existing East Side/West Side binary was open to challenge or change. This evolving discourse signaled to us that possibilities existed for disrupting the historically developed divisions. In effect, we were witness to an evolution in the relations that constitute social space. The assemblage of knowledges, technologies, and practices revealed in these educators' acts made particularly visible that there is considerable agency in the construction of space. It also is a telling example, as we will show, of the ways in which spatialized and spatializing practices are not only linked to historical, social and economic forces, but that they involve individuals' and groups' embodied acts, that space is personalized and invested with personal meanings. As such, Central City schools serve as a window into the negotiation of meaning involved in schools' and educators' response to a major event, as the students and families they encountered were no longer those with whom they had been familiar and comfortable. As we looked deeper, it became clear that these schools represented sites of confrontation and alchemy of competing knowledge frameworks and people.

The Productive Nature of Teachers' and Principals' Discourse

The production of knowledge seen here was even more dramatic than in the East Side and West Side schools, as teachers and principals didn't re-instantiate historically constructed divisions, but instead participated in the production of a new construct and hybrid discourse that was beginning to emerge in this space but outside schools as well (a community center in the area had adopted the name Central City some years before the construct surfaced in school documents). This new code served to identify as unique the space in the Valley that was experiencing the most rapid and recent demographic shift. For the schools in our study, the emergence of this new code begged for us the questions, "What purpose did this new construct serve? What meanings underlie it? Why was it necessary?"

Central City is an area of conflict, convergence, and negotiation—a contested space. The students and families that schools in this space serve now bring unfamiliar languages, sociocultural norms, and practices to these formerly East Side schools. As a result, the roles of teachers and principals are undergoing rapid change, and educators are grappling with language to redefine their personal, professional roles and identities. The fact that the existing binary was not invoked, particularly the West Side category that has historically been attached to people of color, highlights the fact that the binary functions to do more than name students and families; educators also invoked the constructs to identify themselves. Thus, one explanation for the discursive ambiguity found in Central City schools may be that educators were seeking a new code that allowed them to retain their image of themselves as "not West Side." As we show, their responses to the rapid, recent change in their schools involved both nostalgia and resistance, while also naming their students as different than in the recent past. In this chapter, we explore the complicated ways in which the use of spatial/linguistic categories in these schools were operating as educators struggled to respond to changing demographics, as well as the varied choices in literacy programs and clusters across the District. Again, the relations among discourse, practice, and technology are illustrative, in this case of the messiness and dynamism of constituting changing social spaces.

Constructing a New Discursive Code

In the absence of use of the east/west binary, more oblique comments characterized educators' discussions. Though the use of the Central City construct itself was explicit in only a few schools, the discourse to which it referred was shared across all the 8 schools. In particular, educators' ways of talking about students and themselves were consistent, and evoked an emerging but as yet ill-formed collective sense of inhabiting the same physical and social space. As such, this discourse functioned in the same capacity as the East Side and West Side discourses that signaled educators' identification with their students and the attendant purposes of schooling (e.g., academically focused, providing social services). The clarity seen in those discourses was not in evidence in this space given the tensions educators were experiencing as their assumptions about themselves as professionals were challenged as they worked to serve unfamiliar students.

For example, in what may be an attempt at self-definition, teachers at one school cited other, nearby schools as being like them: "One thing I'd like to see is neighborhood, neighboring schools maybe like Elkhorn, Roosevelt, and Alpine meet like once every couple of months on a grade level, you know.... We service similar communities and it might be very interesting to see what's working in their classrooms and their schools, and take some of that information and use it here." These teachers pointed to other schools that fit within the same, unnamed category, as well as within the same geographical area, that seemed to match their image of themselves and their students. The east/west binary was not invoked, however, to name this space or the type of students who make up the communities these schools share. There was also a sense that particular practices were appropriate, or work, for particular communities, so that the Central City space should call up a collection of technologies and knowledge, or information that is effective 'here.' Finally, the notions of 'we' and 'here' contributed as well to an ambiguous but still real sense of sharing a space.

In other Central City schools, both teachers and principals talked vaguely about "in certain school settings," or "this school in particular." In contrast to 'east-' and West Side schools, no spatial signifiers were used that coupled demographics with geography; the focus was on demographics only. The Central City construct did not have a similar chain of signifiers like the East Side (academically able, involved parents) or West Side (immigrant, needy, deficient), or an historical set of relations among discourses, practices, and technologies that defined places and people, because the space to which it referred was in flux. The binary that helped distinguish east from west wasn't seen as appropriate here–those constructs invoked relations that were settled long ago and continually reified in both school and broader city discourses. The changing space of the Central City didn't have that history nor was it referred to in those broader discourses. It is the discursive silence about physical location that indicates that a new code may be necessary for these schools to name themselves within the evolving social space of the Valley. Note the lack of a construct in the following enunciation.

E.P.: I asked people from the state office to come down and talk about test scores for people with the demographics that we had. ... she talked about what they were seeing in schools with demographics like ours. What are some strategies for demographics like this? ... And they said well, you know, for schools like this you score in a range of this to this.

Rather than using the larger east/west discourse, talk such as this pointed vaguely at kinds of students to describe these schools. In addition, a particular range of observed test scores was tied to schools as demographic profiles, coupling technologies of categorizing people by ethnicity or race with those of categorizing schools by achievement ranking. As a result, these schools were becoming spatialized through invoking technologies and knowledge (e.g., strategies) deemed appropriate for 'schools like this.' The discourse is one of turning to data of a particular type to identify a social space that then leads educators to 'strategies,' so that guidance in choosing practices comes from an existing, technical knowledge base rather than relying on themselves or on students and their communities for insight as to how to proceed. A sense that these schools were unsure of how to respond to the new Central City scenario emerges from their language frameworks, as does a sense that they were searching for ways to identify themselves with respect to this new space.

These schools were turning to existing technologies and knowledges at the same time that they were grappling with self-definition in relation to a newly forming space. A hybrid discourse emerged that cobbled together discourses regarding students with discourses regarding the purpose of schooling. That new discourse captured the contested nature of naming this space and its inhabitants, as formerly East Side teachers negotiated the web of relations that connected them to what looked to them, based on the data, like West Side students. The fluidity of this spatializing process is captured in the isolated and infrequent use of the east- or West Side constructs found in one Central City school. This principal did talk explicitly about his school as West Side: "I think if you have a good program and good teachers that attendance shouldn't be a problem. But again, in these West Side schools we have families move, come in, move. There's not anything we can do to control that." However, teachers at that same school confounded this usage when they framed the issue of meeting needs in terms not confined to the east/west binary. One teacher noted, "...we can develop [our] plan to meet our needs here in this population and with the cultures we have and we don't have to worry about you know, the far east side, what their needs are aren't our needs, and the far west side. We have different needs." This teacher explicitly acknowledged that a new space with unique needs existed. Strikingly, she used the existing binary to identify her school as signifying an outlying category. Also clear from this discourse is the move to tie practice to place, a place identified by the 'needs' of the population and cultures 'here.' The unsettled nature of this school's identification of place was paralleled, as shown next, in the hybridized Central City discourse that was characterized by both resistance and nostalgia.

"Where Academics Come First While Nurturing the Whole Child"
Where the East Side schools portrayed themselves as academically focused and those on the West Side focused more on social service issues, the talk of staffs in the Central City indicated that they were trying to maintain an emphasis on academics, while expanding their role to also provide social services. The reference in the above subheading to both academics and the whole child was one school's motto, and exemplified these educators' claims (positive or not) to roles in both academic learning and social welfare. Embedded within this discourse is an implicit concept of student that, like schools' self-definitions, was not yet settled. In contrast to the East Side and West Side students who were affixed explicitly, Central City students were viewed ambiguously as both learners and as people in need of services. That view was a contested one, as educators in these schools repeatedly stated that they were trying to hold onto the academic aspects of their work as they also addressed or resisted other perceived needs:

> Elementary Teacher: Because there's only so much time in the day, and if you give up 45 minutes for a class counseling session, uh or 30 minutes, you've got to take it away from somewhere else. We try not to take it away from reading and math. We try to be very strict on that, but other subjects like social studies and science, they suffer (teacher focus group).

The idea of "giving up" time in the day has a negative tone, evidence that teachers' views of what was appropriate to include in the time they had to work with students were being challenged. What had been a focus on academic learning was having to be modified to attend to relationships with and among students. That attention was perceived in therapeutic terms, as calling for counseling, further evidence that teachers were feeling stress rather than possibility in their work with students with whom they were unfamiliar.

Along with modifying the way time was spent in their classrooms, educators were also resisting the expansion of their work, the redefinition of their mission, and the roles of their schools. Another example from the data captures the sense of tension and conflict:

> Elementary Principal: Most of the responses we got from parents [about after-school programming], they were really looking for child care...And none of the teachers would support it. ... what they've wanted to see after school is academic enrichment (principal interview).

The negotiation with families about what schools were supposed to provide, what practices and technologies were within the purview of the space of school, was complex as assumptions were challenged, attempts to serve explored, and positions staked out. Unlike the negotiations with East Side parents that focused on the academic curriculum, and also unlike interactions with West Side parents that focused on training and social services, Central City exchanges were hybridized, producing a third space in which educators were striving to retain former practices and respond to perceived new needs.

The enunciations that characterized educators' roles coupled nostalgic talk about traditional roles (e.g., the emphasis on math and reading) with worried or defiant talk about needing to respond to other parts of students' lives (i.e., "none of the teachers would support it [child care]"). The absence of the East Side/West Side discourses indicates that these educators were struggling to identify a body of knowledge that helped them to name their roles and those of schools. These new discourses had not crystallized, as of yet, into a bound system of knowledge as they decided how to respond to increasing student diversity.

"Students In This Area are Needier Than Ever Before"

Not only were local discourses being hybridized, so were national discourses, especially about students of color. Elements of the deficit discourse so pervasive in schools identified as west side were deployed in Central City schools, but the knowledge of this space was not directly imported from west side schools. Instead, the staff at all of these schools conceptualized their roles and defined their students in terms that corresponded to the spatial-ontological construct of 'inner-city' and 'at-risk' students. This use of a different set of terms that also served as shorthand for referring to race and class highlighted the tense negotiations teachers and principals seemed to be grappling with, where they invoked nationally salient terms that labeled their students with constructs whose meaning is clear but not stated, but avoided using local constructs that would also situate their schools and themselves spatially. The avoidance of the use of the term West Side and the use instead of 'inner city' and 'at risk' terms allowed them to talk of their students while shielding themselves from being identified as West Side teachers. Personalizing this space, investing it with personal meaning, seemed to mean that educators intentionally avoided using the local construct, given the well-understood but implicit social consequences for their self-identities.

As was the case with their East Side and West Side counterparts, educators in this space of the District invoked constructs that masked the racial and class differences being alluded to, evidence that across the Salt Valley direct reference to racial and class difference was avoided. However, the use of 'inner city' and 'at risk' also signaled that Central City educators were identifying their students in deficit terms, constructing them as lacking, while working to distinguish themselves somehow from West Side educators whose identities were tied to West Side students. In addition, as shown later, there was a pragmatic aspect to calling on the national discourses, as they provided a knowledge base from which to draw to choose 'appropriate' technologies and practices.

Dynamics That Spur Spatialization

Elements of the Central City space that drove spatialization were the recent phenomenon of demographic changes in these schools and educators' discourse about the purposes of schooling that conveyed a sense of nostalgia for students and families they had been accustomed to serving (e.g., East Side). Educators employed a language about themselves and their roles around holding onto norms of respect, structure, and a valuing of education in the face of neglect of such mores in students' homes. Teachers, in particular, enunciated a discourse that proffered that there was a lack of home structure and familial support in students' lives, hence, rendering students "at risk." In addition, teachers highlighted the recency of the changes to an "inner city" space and, more importantly, student:

> Elementary Teacher 5: ...the one big thing I've seen a difference is in the kids from there [8 years ago] to now – because it's the same kind of, you know, inner city

kinds of kids – is they really lack reasoning skills now, where before they were low but it was like they had reasoning skills and they could kind of predict some things...
E.T. 6: Yeah, but now everybody has more of them, eight or nine of them instead of one or two.

While the category West Side was not a part of the discourse of these teachers, the spatial-ontological category of "inner city" served a similar purpose in indexing an unstated set of knowledge propositions. The assumption is that all parties know what 'kinds of kids' are referred to by 'inner city.' However, these teachers also provide a temporal dimension with the terms 'now' and 'today,' highlighting the sense that they have experienced a recent change in student body to children who are 'inner city.' Thus, increases in students from communities of color pushed educators to name them, and the choices they made in that naming were an important element in educators' spatializing the newly forming area. In this way, Central City was not named within the historical discourses of the Valley, but instead was named using national discourses that indicated a particular ontology for students and that were more detached from educators themselves.

Principals at these schools also worked from this knowledge base. The same discourses of "inner-city" parents and the roles of inner-city schools were generally prevalent in principals' talk.

> Elementary Principal: ...our families are so limited in what they can give. Um, because they work two jobs, or because they don't speak English, they're limited ...it's as if schools or kids have to be able to succeed without their family, in a way.
> E.P.: There's a whole world of incompetent parents out there. Somehow parenting seems to have disappeared. It's sort of that attitude, 'we brought 'em into the world, now they're yours. Do something with them.'

Overall, these statements highlight the point that the identification as an 'inner-city' school is not solely a geographical positioning, but also an ontological signifier used to represent student demographics that carries with it specific types of pedagogical and curricular exigencies, and knowledge about the inner-city student and family. Educators within the Central City corridor suggest that being an inner-city school is a social and spatial condition that was brought about with the arrival of particular families. These educators still articulated, however, a discourse of nostalgia where they envisioned their role as merely educating children and not engaging in what they termed 'social work.'

Importantly, educators' reaching outside the space of the Valley to national discourses that also spatialize practices based on deficit notions about students and families of color served to limit the possibilities for novel responses to change. Thus instead of pointing to responses that could lead to new relationships among knowledge, practices, and technologies, this Central City discourse seemed to be aligning itself with the West Side space in terms of views of students at the same time as it struggled with teacher identity as not-West Side. The East Side and West Side educators' use of local constructs to identify students was coupled with calling up of particular knowledge, technologies and practices in their particular spaces, explored below in their choices of literacy programs and school clusters. Because of the tension in the Central City space, evidenced in educators' using national constructs to identify students but not themselves, such coupling was much more difficult. Given the ambiguity found in the talk of teachers and principals at Central City schools, we turned to these schools' improvement plans (documents required as part of a whole-District reform effort) and to the literacy programs and clusters they chose to focus on emergent categories being used to define students and schools' purposes. Not surprisingly, given the complexity inherent in crafting a new self-identifying category within the larger community, national and historical discourse, confusing patterns emerged in these analyses.

School Improvement Plans

The categories of East- and West Side were not invoked anywhere in these documents, consistent with the patterns in educators' discourse. Instead, our analysis of the plans revealed that the Central City schools either did not invoke any category (two schools), or they named themselves using terms other than East or West Side. In three schools, the signifier inner city is linked to ethnicity/race, poverty, language, and instability, similar to the West Side code. Most interesting in terms of local dynamism in spatial/linguistic constructs, in two school improvement plans the term Central City is prominent in the self-definitions: "located on the edge of Central City," and "an elementary school located in the Central City area." One of the schools placed its street address in the same sentence in which the term Central City was invoked, using one as a marker for the other, helping the reader locate the school and "Central City" geographically. In addition, the student population was described as "neighborhood" versus "magnet gifted and talented," with text helping to clarify to whom Central City refers:

"While most children walk to school, the magnet program has students carpooled from all over the city." The other school followed its use of the term Central City with detailing the movement of students in and out of the school: "Between 150-170 students transfer to [School] each year, with most coming from [three other Central City schools]. Between 120-150 students transfer to other schools, with the largest percentages attending [two East Side schools]." Again, this use of Central City as a category was accompanied with discursive markers to alert the reader as to where the school was and that Central City students were arriving and East Side students were leaving. As such, the category was being defined by both place and the descriptions of people who inhabited it, coupling mobility with the Central City term. The term was used much less widely within institutional spaces (e.g., schools) in comparison to the media. Thus, in schools, it seemed to be a locally developing code that may serve, some day, as a third signifier to characterize both a part of the city and the inhabitants therein.

Spatialized and Spatializing Technologies of Central City

A feature of both the reform and of the requirements schools had to address for state and federal funding involved categorizing students according to race, ethnicity, socioeconomic status, and English language proficiency. As stated in Chapter 4, the technologies of counting and funding based on those counts spatialized East Side and West Side schools in particular ways; the same is the case in Central City. However, given the dynamic evolution of this space, these technologies served to constrain possibilities for disrupting the historical division in the Valley and in Salt Lake Valley schools. All the schools qualified for Title I and Highly Impacted Schools funds, so that the existing federal and state apparatuses pushed schools into using the existing logic of deficit based on race and class. The reform's requirement that schools describe their students using the same terms and that achievement data had to be disaggregated along those same lines reinforced that logic (and that of the soon-to-be enacted No Child Left Behind legislation).

Of course, schools need money to fund programs and to buy curricula, and serving growing numbers of students who are English language learners and/or lack of financial resources is a challenge for schools. Still, the coupling of 'at risk' to students' culture, race, and language in a de facto way limits the ways that students and families of color can participate and be viewed. This constrains the types of programs, relationships, and sources of information treated as legitimate (e.g., not the families or communities), and naturalizes deficit-based, remediation-focused programming. As a result, Central City's potential as a space of freedom (see Foucault, 1988) was limited by the funding formulas and reform mandates that re-instantiated the historical divisions in the Valley, that failed to problematize the identification of groups of people as normal/different or able/unable, and that offered time-worn guidance on which programs 'naturally' belong in particular spaces.

Literacy Programs

The ambiguity in educators' discourse and the ways that schools described themselves in school improvement plans was mirrored in the choices of technologies of schooling and reform made by educators in the Central City area. Schools adopted a variety of literacy programs that ranged from the rigidly scripted SFA and CEL/xLL curricula to more flexible programs such as the Scholastic literacy program and the Literacy For All (LFA) program that was constructed by schools on the East Side. Looking across the adoptions, there appeared to be a strong relationship between the discourses circulating within these schools about students and families and their adoption of particular literacy programs. The schools in Central City that aligned themselves with the SFA and CEL/xLL shared a similar knowledge base as West Side schools who framed students as 'needy' and as 'socially deficit,' whereas schools who participated in the LFA program with schools on the east side of the city enunciated a complex discourse that emphasized, at times, the 'at-risk' status of students but also the need to connect the curricula to the strengths and insights that students and families brought to school. Note the differences in tone in the following excerpts from, first, two schools that adopted a rigidly scripted program also found in West Side schools, and second, two schools that adopted the more balanced, less prescriptive programs found on the East Side:

> Principal: I've decided that one of the things is, at this school in particular, there are so many social services issues… I think some of them [teachers] are barely keeping their head above water just dealing with kids, there are so many critical issues here. (Elementary principal)
> Teacher: Somehow parenting seems to have disappeared. … And that means everything. … We opened the door, took responsibility away from the parents and the learning and teaching is suffering. (Elementary teacher)

Also:

> Teacher 1: The thing is you really can't learn about a culture, or really know a culture until you've been in it and you've been there. I mean you can read about it but that's not the same as actually being there and being a part of it.
> T5: I don't know if that's our job either. Just teaching more acceptance.
> T1: I see myself—our job is to teach them how to function in our society and also our society to function in a world society where everybody needs to work together and if we can get them to accept other's differences but to learn how to live within this society I think you're going to be—
> T2: I think we're kind of missing the boat because we have some experts in the parents, in the children, and we're missing the boat because we're not using our experts to help us to understand what diversity is all about, what acceptance is all about. (Elementary teachers)

The conflicting messages in the second group of teachers' talk, all of whom taught together, highlighted the nature of the identity work educators were engaged in as they grappled with knowing their students, reconfiguring their roles, and reconsidering the purpose of schooling. It may be that the mixture of both positive and deficit discourses regarding the communities they were serving, along with their sense of themselves as 'not West Side,' influenced their decisions to adopt a less structured literacy program that kept open the possibility that they could still be 'experts' who make professional judgments rather than implementers of teacher-proof curricula. These contradictions and tensions in the relations among discourse, practice, and technologies in the evolving Central City area illuminate the messiness and dynamism of the production of space.

School Clusters

While the literacy programs and the accompanying clustering of schools functioned to render the spatio-ontological constructs of the East Side and the West Side as salient knowledge, the Central City schools did not have a third option in the clustering that reflected their contexts, even though they saw themselves as not clearly East Side or West Side schools. They did not recognize each other as a collective, either, that had shared interests and student populations around which they could craft or choose a literacy program. These schools were forced, instead, into the binary that existed, clustering with either East Side or West Side schools. Five of the schools adopted the SFA or the CEL/xLL program and participated in clusters with schools that identified themselves as West Side schools. These five summoned the knowledge of West Side students as deficit, as uninterested, and as at-risk to talk about their students. Reasons for choosing these clusters centered on finding–"other schools doing what we wanted to do ... we share training costs" (principal interview)–thereby both identifying themselves with West Side schools' technologies and practices, and sharing resources or reducing costs. Connected to educators' use of national discourses of students of color as 'at risk' and 'inner city,' these schools were able to accomplish pragmatic things in terms of deciding how to allocate resources based on the direction the use of those constructs provided about choices of 'appropriate' programs. Importantly, they also placed themselves within the spatial relations forged through discourse, practice, and technology that located them with others they perceived as having similar students and purposes.

The three remaining schools within the Central City corridor who aligned themselves with the clusters composed of schools on the East Side summoned, as we have mentioned, a complex knowledge base to talk about their practice and their students. While their discourses about their students were tied to national discourses of 'at risk' and 'inner city,' their choice of cluster placed them with East Side schools, creating some tension among discourse, practices, and technology. One principal indicated how the decision to join those schools was made: "so many of the schools in [the literacy cluster] have a unique approach that works for them." She then contrasted the less prescriptive, teacher-created approach in this program to the more scripted programs that required a strict structure and consistency across grade levels that was "not for them." In addition, these principals conferred with each other and with a district person who "interviewed us and thought we'd be a great fit, " a clear indicator of being identified and identifying themselves as "like" East Side schools. This hybrid discourse was made up of those found in schools on the West Side (at risk, deficit-based) as well as on the East Side (rejecting rigid literacy programs). Thus, the choice to cluster embedded these schools in complex and contradictory spatial relations.

Summary

The material relations among discourse, technologies, and practice in this area of the Valley show more fluidity, tension, and negotiation than those in the other two areas. In particular, the durability of the West Side construct seems to be challenged when educators are faced with applying the term to themselves. Central City teachers' and principals' use of nationally significant rather than locally constructed terms that serve as shorthand for deficit-based markers for race and class makes clear the spatial features of this space. The messy, ambiguous, complex assemblages of discourses, technologies, and practices seen across the eight Central City schools reflect the tense and contested nature of this social space. Educators did not align themselves with their students in the way that West Side teachers did, but instead exhibited resistance and nostalgia in their negotiation of this newly emerging social and physical space. Such resistance and reflection on identity, practices, and purposes did not characterize, for the vast majority, their negotiations regarding their students, though. Given the existing logic underlying the technologies of schooling and reform, along with the prevailing local and national knowledge frameworks or discourses about students and families of color, opportunities and impetus to question the portrayal of the unfamiliar students arriving in their buildings were largely absent.

CHAPTER 6

THE DURABILITY AND FLUX
OF LOCAL SPATIAL KNOWLEDGE

The picture that we have presented in this book is one of a spatial educational knowledge that has worked in concert with various technologies to produce differentiated educational subjects and schools across Salt Valley City. The local knowledge circulating within city relations and the schools is an important element in shaping the urban landscape of people, buildings and neighborhoods. It weighed heavily on how individuals imagined and organized the space of the city and its schools. This knowledge came to play in helping those within the dominant network of relations to denote official meanings about the criminal, the civic minded, the at-risk and the normal, as well as the spaces of desirability and undesirability.

In this chapter, we discuss the findings of the spatial knowledge that is produced within city schools. We first theorize the presence and power, or effects, of local spatial knowledge and its production by teachers within the school district. We contemplate why this local knowledge functioned as an epistemological base for educators. We further link this knowledge to that which circulates within the city to discuss the space producing function of this knowledge. This conversation discusses how schools should be seen as key participants in propelling segregated city spaces, rather than just the effects of city processes of segregation and differentiation. We argue that the designation of schools as West Side and East Side, as well as their respective assemblage of curricular programs, become important factors that shape the demographics of the city's real estate markets. The conversation then turns to a discussion of the durability and change of this knowledge. Specifically, we proffer a theory of why this knowledge maintained its continuity, as well as experienced a rupture through the emergence of the Central City construct. Finally, we lay out recommendations for addressing the tensions of knowledge production and representation within schools and cities.

Spatiality of Institutional Knowledge

Current academic discussions about the effects of the language and requirements of national policy documents—such as No Child Left Behind—on educators' practices have prompted many in the field to focus their attention on these macro-policies and structures (McNeil, 2000; Valenzuela, 2003). Many have sought especially to understand how these national initiatives affect urban schools that have a long history of racial segregation and patterns of differentiated curriculum. What we need to add to these rich analyses is the power of local systems of knowledge as well as the local landscape of city structural arrangements in shaping how educators envision their students, their work, and their social space. Much of the educational research focused on urban education has given methodological primacy to structural ecological relations (i.e., housing, suburbanization trends). The realm of knowledge has been relegated to the background of the city's social fields. Our examination suggests that local knowledge matters greatly in the production and enactment of educators' practices. The local knowledge of the East Side, West Side, and Central City student and school served in Salt Valley Schools as an epistemological base for educators in defining their students and their work. It was the reigning logic for naming, knowing and ordering (i.e., organizing) school bodies, places and materials. Similar, in some senses, to what Popkewitz's (1998B) and McDermott's (1996) studies found, the knowledge base underpinning educators' understanding of the ontology of their students, students' academic and social needs, and their own work as teachers and principals was entangled with these local, historical, and spatial discourses of student, teaching and schooling.

To elaborate on this entanglement, the local socio-historical discourses of the West Side and East Side student and family had achieved the status of a régime of truth (Foucault, 1978) across the city and its schools. The historical spatial and racial meanings of city residents and places that circulated amongst the media and political relations in the city had an air of common sense and truthfulness within schools. There was a high degree of continuity between the meanings, or discourses, that educators employed and those in circulation across different historical periods and spaces. Our discussion will take up the durability of these constructs shortly, but permit us to state at this point that the prominence and dispersion of this knowledge in the city, as well as the practices deployed in schools, constrained educators' frameworks largely to the local knowledge of the city when discussing their students, their schools and themselves as educators. While there was certainly articulation of these local discourses within national conversations of such things as the 'at risk,' 'the poor,' and 'minority,' our analyses showed that the local was the most salient in the differentiation of spaces, people and practices across the Valley's elementary schools.

The media and other local conversations, both within and outside of schools, as well as the built environment kept these constructs and their meanings at the center of the dominant knowledge frameworks of the city and its subjects. The historical racial and class denoting representations of city subjects that were instantiated in the media and by local politicians were pervasive and retained a general coherence in the professional frameworks of educators from East Side and West Side schools. Discursive elements were shared between the city's media, politicians and educators as each entity's conversations about these places and subjects overlapped with each other's language.

This injunction of discourse through the interconnection of spatial relations (i.e., schools, media, city leaders) demonstrates empirically how objects, bodies, structures and knowledge come to work as networked spatial relations, an argument put forward by theorists such as Foucault (1978) and Popkewitz (1998B), among others (see Butler, 1999). Spatial relations take up and are inscribed with a discourse that parallels the logic of other relations, creating a dialogic relationship of shared signifiers and meanings (i.e., knowledge) (Buendía, 2002). Material objects are simultaneously organized to function from this system of reasoning, through the interlocking of objects, bodies, knowledge and built environments through practice. Because the language and meanings of the media, politicians and schools paralleled each other so closely, most residents and educators were unable to recognize the seams between one relation and another. This may be due to the amalgamation of these various relations over time and through practice (Bourdieu, 1990). Conflicting purposes or aims between institutional relations are resolved as the common discursive framework of the East Side and West Side provides a common logic to the structural organization of the city.

The social and historical status of these spatial categories as shared local knowledge is important as we consider what was obscured when they were employed in their shorthand form. The ability of educators to use the shorthand to name racial and social class meanings, even in ways that might be perceived as genteel, hid the productive and reproductive dimensions of educational practice as they pertained to race and social class. It allowed educators to produce and index racial and classed meanings of city subjects and spaces (i.e., school and city) without explicitly employing politically charged terms. These discursive practices permitted them to appear, at one level, color- and class-blind in their production and enactment of pedagogical knowledge, while their patterns of curricular distinctions were based on racial and class meanings that were hidden by these codes. To put this differently, explicit references to race and class were missing from public view, yet they were omnipresent through the constructs and the historical and contemporary meanings that have underpinned them.

In identifying the productive and shared qualities of this knowledge about race, space and educating, we need to clarify our argument that the production of these meanings at the level of schools was not unidirectional or solely mimetic. A clear illustration of this process was evident in the appropriation of federal educational discourse and the construction of a new construct, the Central City student and school. These events demonstrated how educators participated in the production of a city knowledge of subjects and places. We saw in these how educators in Salt Valley School District were active agents in the production of the East Side, West Side and Central City knowledge. What they constructed, however, was an institutionally specific strand of educational knowledge of the subject and of educating. While it overlapped closely with the racial and classed meanings that already had a historical presence in the media and in the discussions of politicians, the institutional nuances centered on individual and group cognitive ability, educational history, the social capital that different populations of parents brought—or lacked—to the realm of schools and education, as well as their pedagogical and curricular needs. These elements of this discourse differed slightly from the media and politicians' conversations of criminality and cleanliness. Where they overlapped, however, was in the references to particular racial and spatial populations and their alleged civil traits, or lack thereof.

We should view these nuances in teachers' and principals' discursive practices as supplementing the citywide representations with additional meanings of East Side and West Side subjects' educational past, present and future. From one vantage point, it appeared that there was no difference in the language frames of educators and, say, the media. The similarity of this knowledge to those discourses already in play in dominant spatial relations allowed many residents–those who had not considered or questioned these meanings–to recognize these codes as having a real, material correspondence to particular spatialized subjects. In other words, educators' practices of naming schools as East Side or West Side helped to move these codes from the realm of the imaginary and the constructed to that of the material and the natural. The pervasiveness of these overlapping discourses relegated the challenges to the dominant discourse, such as those comments by residents from the western side of the city pertaining to the freeway construction, to the periphery of conversations about these spaces.

Yet differences in the discourses of different relations did exist. The seams in the discourses were evident if one looked closely at the nuances in the terms of the West Side and East Side. What appears to explain the distinctive elements in educators' discourse is the fact that they produced and instantiated this knowledge and practice of differentiated educational backgrounds, capabilities and aspirations amidst somewhat different, yet interrelated, spatial relations than those of other city entities, such as the media and politicians. These involved, in part, common elements such as the historical knowledge of the city, its residents, and the ecological organization of the city. There were other institutionally specific spatial relations such as federal funding apparatuses, historical socio-psychological discourses of the at-risk and the normal, as well as objects such as curricular materials and pedagogical structures (e.g., literacy programs and clusters). Many of these are inherent to educational institutions of educating within the United States and the West (Tyack & Cuban, 1995). Others, on the other hand, are localized city relations that had been coupled to processes of educating within particular parts of the city.

The Knowledge of Difference and School Re-segregation

This production and obscuring of these meanings of the West Side, East Side and Central City through the integration of people, discourse and structures has a great deal of import as we put into play the local and national pattern of segregated neighborhoods and re-segregated schools (see Lipman, 2002; Kantor & Brenzel 1993; Orfield, 1996). While educators' social context of city relations produced class- and race-defining practices—particularly in the patterns of segregated housing and the structuring of federal and state educational funding targeted at non-white, low-income families—teachers' and principals' production and use of these shorthand constructs allowed them to maintain that they did not exacerbate these patterns by differentiating the curriculum based on deficit conceptions that were premised on racial or classed constructions of students. Their practices created an illusion of being positioned outside of the social processes of differentiations based on race and class. The practice of employing the shorthand allowed them to make distinctions based on the composite the West Side or East Side student. This allowed them to negate as well as reinforce the pattern of hyper-segregation around race that was in place in the city. This negation involved the explicit hiding of race behind spatial metaphors, such that race was rarely mentioned pointedly. On the other hand, these practices reinforced the city's hyper-segregation by re-ordering curricula, people and fiscal resources in ways that reproduced the historical patterns of differentiated curricula, or low status knowledge for students of color who are concentrated in one part of the city and high status for the white population located in another. Furthermore, these practices locked people into social relationships where conversations about race were divided into binaries of the white/Latino, the intellectually ready/not ready, and the East Side/West Side.

A question that begs to be discussed is why schools and urban communities disguise conversations about race in such a fashion. Our sense is that we can read these practices of obscuring race as a contemporary instantiation of what Gregory Jacobs (1998) and Thomas and Mary Edsall (1992) refer to as the new symbolic language of the politics of race. Where social scientists such as Robert Park and, later, politicians historically codified black people and spaces with scientific constructs and terms such as the "ghetto" or "busing" to indirectly name and manage race (see Ward, 1989)–or conjure up specific meanings about it, without ever uttering the term explicitly–Salt Valley educators' institutional use of the West Side and East Side constructs functioned the same way. Their deployment of these constructs was propelled by pragmatic purposes as well as a historical project of racial and class differentiation that has been hidden by conversations of meeting "needs" and student difference. The need to name place and subjects is an inherent function in constructing practices within schools, a theme that we will elaborate on a bit later as we discuss the durability of this knowledge. Furthermore, the racial politics of the city and the country (US) has been one of continual racial differentiation while exceedingly hiding the explicit mentioning of race (Omi & Winant, 1991). This has been especially true in the post-civil rights era where many public institutions have deemed the social differentiation around race as remedied and an antiquity of the past, and have engaged in removing references to race from public policy and practice (for a discussion see Orfield, 1996). Yet, historical meanings of race have prevailed through subtleties in the terms employed to discuss it in the public sphere.

This argument parallels one we have posed elsewhere, that policy discourses built on a color-blind definition of the individual (e.g., NCLB, advocacy in Salt Valley District) mask the influence of historical and present-day race relations in the spaces of schools (Ares & Buendía, Forthcoming). We can extend that argument of masking and shaping to include shorthand constructs that spatialize discourse, practice, knowledge, and technologies. As George Carew (1997) notes, liberal views that focus on individualism claim that the pursuit of equity must be grounded in policies that transcend group difference. However, attempts at transcendence ignore the fact that "racialized discourses are inescapable in US schooling, given its history as a public institution and its role in the development of a multicultural society" (Ares & Buendía, Forthcoming). As such, the Central City, East Side, and West Side constructs cloak the inevitable influence of race relations on the production of knowledge, technologies, and practice, and the creation and maintenance of differentiated spaces of schooling. Further, they constrain educators' disruption of the West Side/East Side binary, as seen in Central City teachers' and principals' deficit-based, West Side discourses about their students. Similar to color-blind policies existing in a society that still marks subjects through racial distinctions, these constructs prevent teachers and principals from moving outside the liberal individualistic "rhetoric … [that] is commonly used as a pretext to continue to justify hierarchical racial divisions" (Parker, 2002, p. 150).

The Active Production of Space

While educators participated in the construction of a differentiated student ontology, we have also shown how and argued that the production of knowledge and the coordination of technologies produced space, particularly differentiated educational institutions. Educators organized and invested themselves, as well as the technologies at hand, employing the logic underpinning the knowledge of the East Side, West Side and Central City space and subject. The interplay of this knowledge with the pre-existing and newly introduced technologies of schools secreted, as Henri Lefebvre (1991) would say, spaces of difference. The spatial differentiation involved building and fortifying environments, or places, with an array of technologies (e.g., from funding to curriculum), spatio-bodily relations (e.g., identification of and alignment with other East Side or West Side schools) and practices (e.g., organizing and meeting in clusters). These spatial productions came to be represented as East Side, West Side or Central City schools and subjects. This cultural and material production and reproduction of distinct educational populations and school spaces corresponded to the historical material relations constituting the city geography, as well as the general meanings that have been applied historically to different spaces and people of the city. This coordination naturalized the city's geographical division by re-institutionalizing spatially distinct school spaces that mapped directly onto the broader divisions of the city. Educators' usage and investment in this spatial and spatializing knowledge transformed these imagined spaces into distinct educational places, in terms of the organization of pedagogy, curriculum and constituents (i.e., families, students, and teachers). Our use of the construct place is employed here to emphasize the processes of historical construction by the people who reside and engage in practices of life amidst diverse relations; places are, as Margaret Rodman (2003) defines, "politicized, culturally relative, historically specific, local and multiple constructions" (p. 205).

These acts of producing and reproducing differentiated places in Salt Valley School District parallel, to some degree, the findings of other studies. For example, this can be found in the context that Angela Valenzuela (1999) studied in documenting the subtractive practices of East End schools in Houston, Texas, as well as Jonathan Kozol's (1992) multi-city (US based) examination. Both referred to patterns of spatial differentiation in the distribution of funding and curricular technologies across city spaces, even though the production of space was not a focal point of their analyses. Race was a central element in these processes of differentiation as white, middle- and upper-class students received different financial allocations and experienced other types of pedagogies than the black and Latina/o students in other parts of the city. Because the relationship between space, subjects and knowledge distribution is not a focus in these studies, these authors left unexplored the broader, citywide meanings of city spaces and particular populations that were entangled with the rationales informing the organization of resources in schools on the East End of Houston or East St. Louis.

A study that takes up explicitly the question of space and the production of particular educational populations is Pauline Lipman's (2002) analysis of Chicago's policies of school and program placement within the city. Her findings parallel our argument about the production of space. She found that the curricular policies of the city mayor's office were creating different types of institutions across the city that catered to different racial and class populations. The mayor's office located compensatory programs within neighborhoods with large numbers of Latina/o and black students while it established college track programs in white, affluent areas of the city. Similar to what this book reports, Lipman concluded that these decisions reproduced the geographical divisions as well as the class and race relations of city residents that have existed historically within Chicago. The thoroughness and richness of Lipman's analysis and data allows us to see how schools work to attract and repel populations to particular places of the city.

In all of these studies a pattern that is omnipresent is that particular types of educational practices and technologies can be found in consolidated city segments, or patches of neighborhoods. Neighborhoods identified as "poverty areas" (Neckerman & Wilson, 1988), or locales with students who are poor and of color, were more likely than other parts of the city to have school programs that are compensatory in nature. Distinct spatialized pedagogies and practices can be found. However, in the few studies that tie city processes and relations to these school practices (cf. Kantor & Brenzel, 1993; Kozol, 1992), schools are generally theorized as epiphenomena of the social ecology (e.g., housing and demographic patterns of cities) of the city. Researchers, in other words, have positioned schools conceptually within a hierarchical, unidirectional relationship, where the programs and practices found in schools are determined by the city's social ecology and/or the policies of state legislators.

We would like to revise this argument, to some degree. We want to argue that the creation of schools with these differentiated programs has a more interactive role with the landscape of cities than initially theorized. In placing schools back into the fray of housing markets, we want to push our analysis and interpretation of data and argue that the spatial meanings and material differentiations that educators produce about themselves, their students, and space greatly affects the social ecology of cities. These practices contribute to exacerbating housing segregation (Morantz, 1996). The knowledge and practices that schools produce and become known for becomes an important variable in propelling housing segregation within the city.

Our argument is premised on the pattern that real estate values are determined, in part, by school reputation (Morantz, 1996; Jacobs, 1998). The public's perception of schools has partly driven where individuals with a fair amount of capital purchase their homes (Jackson, 1985), particularly white buyers who do not face racial steering. For example, Gregory Jacobs (1998) identified how community perceptions of Columbus City schools, beginning in the 1970s, shaped the development of single family housing in Columbus, Ohio. He reports that as city educators and the school board discussed possibilities of desegregation and busing, politicians and white real estate agents branded Columbus inner-city schools with racially encoded terms, such as "urban" and as a "bussing" district. Real estate agents, developers, lending institutions and residents all fled to the city's suburbs, fearing schools would be populated by black children. The processes of desegregation of schools had not even begun when the flight began. Schools and the school board were merely discussing these ideas. Yet, the building within and selling of the suburbs exploded as a result of these institutional conversations and the fear that ensued. Alison Morantz's (1996) examination of the Charlotte-Mecklenburg School system (North Carolina, USA) also supports this position in noting that schools were fueling housing segregation, rather than vice versa. Hence, schools, too, are key players in shaping what the dominant deems as the spaces of desirability and undesirability within cities.

We can interpret a similar effect within Salt Valley Schools. Educators' production and institutionalization of the West Side and East Side constructs has an unintentional sway on defining what parts of the city are desirable and undesirable areas. Educators do this by participating in defining and structuring the hierarchy of "at risk" and "low performing" schools and populations. They participate in naming populations and structuring school processes such that particular schools teach an enriched curricula while others deliver a compensatory one, as we showed in the choices of literacy programs across the Valley. Much of this is embedded in naming their populations with descriptors as stable or unstable, or as bringing, or lacking, assets to the enterprise of education. Much has been written on the reproduction of low achievement and compensatory educational programs, particularly the way that standardized tests and funding mechanisms propel a defensive curricula and pedagogy (see McNeil, 2000; Valenzuela, 1996). These processes work in concert with the meanings that dominate in the media and that circulate within particular community groups. Media, real estate agents and banks translate these meanings as "safe" and "desirable" neighborhoods (Jacobs, 1998; Jackson, 1985). Within Salt Valley, census records report a racial divide that falls along the lines of the East Side and

West Side division (Kantor, 2003). That is, city areas the media and other city relations deem as safe (i.e., East Side) are populated by the white middle class, whereas those inscribed as dangerous and as having less value, and identified as West Side, are composed primarily of Latina/os, Tongans, Vietnamese and working class whites.

In arguing that educators are participants in the production of segregated city spaces our intent is not to completely downplay the economic backdrop that shapes the choices of neighborhood that some people have. The fact that the majority of Latina/os and recent immigrants and refugees fall into the ranks of the working class greatly shaped their housing options (Kantor, 2003). However, the entanglement of this economic backdrop with the institutional and citywide meanings of people and the places where they reside functioned hand-in-hand to portray a troubling picture of these places and these populations as desirable and undesirable. The effect of these representations and technologies is a crystallization of different spaces that are segregated such that the white middle and elite class opt for any other place to live than the West Side.

Durability Through Reinstantiation

In discussing this school knowledge as a contemporary instantiation of the new vocabulary of the politics of race, we have to acknowledge that this knowledge is not necessarily new. Rather, it needs to be remembered that these discourses are historical. We have noted that there has been a great deal of continuity in this citywide discourse over time and across various institutional spaces. This durability can be explained by theorizing the formation of these constructs as assemblages of discourse, practices, and material relations that helped not only to build but also to sustain these constructs. Although the knowledge of the East and West Side has many parallels to other national discourses about difference (i.e., historical deficit discourses, nativist and immigrant discourses), its enduring power continues, in large part, because it has existed locally over time and functioned at the level of daily practice to help educators and city dwellers make sense of and manage their local space. The everyday, personal nature of this local knowledge bolsters its durability and its seeming naturalness. It also diminishes the opportunities for reflection on its content and implications, given the implicit and familiar dimensions of these shorthand referents.

While the historical, economic and personal dimensions function to sustain this knowledge, we have to wonder how the built environment of the city also reflects and propels the practices of difference and division. It could be argued that residents' repeated activity amidst the city's buildings, parks, railroad lines, industrial, residential and commercial centers also buttressed these differences. Practices such as crossing the tracks to get from one side of the city to the other, negotiating the freeway's elevated support walls that cut across the city, driving on the freeway and viewing what seems to be two distinct places, and naming different parts of the city using distinct spatial signifiers may also continuously fortify the symbolic meanings of these spaces as well as the types of activities that can occur in particular spaces. The historical and contemporary systems of representation, the built environment, and the routines of daily life may have constrained the degree to which residents can imagine and act within particular places. Furthermore, the interplay of these realms (i.e., the representational, the built, and the practiced) seems to be inclined towards creating coherence, or the appearance of a settled social order (Lefebvre, 1991), between the uses and life trajectories of the objects and people that reside in these spaces.

The durability of this knowledge within the city's schools is also hinged on the relationship between spatial knowledge, built school environments in the form of educational technologies and institutional practices. While schools were situated within spatial relationships historically identified as the West Side and the East Side, educators continuously engaged in practices that re-asserted these knowledge frameworks. We showed, in previous chapters, how this historical knowledge and various educational apparatuses shaped new reforms, as in the adoption of literacy technologies. New technologies were assembled to work within the established meanings that circulated historically, spatially, and in concert with pre-existing technologies. They were spatialized so that they fit the perceived logic of place and subject. Educators' practices, such as the analysis of data disaggregated according to race and class (paralleling mandates in No Child Left Behind), the act of choosing literacy programs based on those analyses and their sense of who they and their students were, and the clustering of schools according to literacy program adoption bolstered the constructs' durability as objects and people were coordinated to fit within the dominant institutional logic of place and population.

The significance of this process of spatialization was that it retained local practices of representing race and class as it coordinated new objects and bodies. The meanings of particular groups were re-inscribed with language that reasserted differences, or discursive divisions, between spaces and people. The implications of these processes of spatialization were that they not only become the symbolic terms for which people were represented, but they also came to play in how individuals were received and responded to within institutions. In other words, discourse came between people in their interactions with each other. Just as Nancy Fraser (1989) found that men and women have differential rights in the social welfare system due to the manner in which policy texts socially constructed them, our study found that students and families had differential rights to education across the space of the Valley. Based on the knowledge of East and West Side subject, individuals were positioned as either clients (West Side) who needed to be treated or co-participants (East Side) who were active, capable agents in their own education.

The situating of "East Siders" as co-participants was predicated on the racial invisibility that was rendered to them through the processes of inscription. Others have discussed how a central attribute of whiteness is the lack of needing to define itself (McIntyre, 1997; Morrison, 1992). The articulation of the East Side was enacted through a similar process of silence about itself, even as the practices of the East Side inscribed a self–other relationship in deeming who were the needy and the normal. "West Siders," on the other hand, were reduced, institutionally, to stated and inferred tropes around race and class that have had a long persistence in local and national history (see Perea, 1997). The premise that these students and families were more than just racialized and classed subjects never emerged institutionally.

Disjuncture and Contested Space

The ambiguity in the Central City schools' discourses and practices provides a vivid example of the constructed nature of the spatial knowledge embodied in the East Side, West Side codes. Central City educators' use of nationally prominent, rather than locally constructed, terms as shorthand for race and class makes clear the disjuncture, or slippage, in the knowledge base as the East–West binary was placed in tension in these schools. The tension is clear in the conflicting ways that teachers talked about themselves and their schools (i.e., ambiguous), the technologies they chose (i.e., East or West Side), and the ways they talked about students (i.e., inner-city). In other words, the disjuncture in the Central City space was focused on educators' struggles to craft new spatialized professional identities without problematizing the naming and treatment of their students. Our data show that teachers in the Central City schools were clinging tightly to historical, nostalgic notions of their work and their mission, while resisting both the East Side and West Side label as a self-referent. As a result, they drew on the only other language frameworks readily available—national discourses of at-risk and urban—when local discourses were unacceptable. National and local discourses co-mingled and influenced practice and knowledge; however, the nature of those national discourses is such that the knowledge embodied in them constrained possibilities for practice and technologies in ways that were similar to the local constructs.

We should read what is transpiring in Central City schools as acts of contestation, that is, as educators struggling with the knowledge frameworks and technologies that are available. This struggle and ambiguity in the Central City space may lead to possibilities of a new institutional category and practices that might blur the East Side–West Side dichotomy. The hybridization of East and West Side frameworks that was enacted in this space may afford educators and students opportunities to engage in learning and interactions that are inclusive of divergent ways of being and learning that are less constrained than those in East Side or West Side schools. However, for alternative pedagogies to emerge, educators must continue to scrutinize and negate the prevailing binary that is incited by peers in other schools as well as in new technologies, such as reform initiatives. They may have to identify other knowledge frameworks that define families and students differently than do the knowledge frameworks currently in circulation in these various institutional spaces. They may have to rely on other sources, such as families and communities, to define the frameworks and funds of knowledge (Gonzalez, Andrade, Civil, & Moll, 2001; McKay & Wong, 1996) that contest particular institutional framings. Important models of such alternatives may already exist in Afro-centric schools and other alternative educational spaces such as Bob Moses' Algebra Project in Boston.

We are cautious, however, in deeming the Central City schools as an example of what might be interpreted as spaces of freedom. The Valley's spatial and historical features weigh heavily on our theorizing for claiming such a thesis. Alternative practices are contingent on the availability of alternative knowledge frameworks as well as other technologies that can propel ambiguity and new pedagogical formulations. There are no guarantees, as alternatives can also mask and index historical meanings of race and class. The conversion of space into place suggests that particular possibilities are foreclosed as educators attempt to designate and manage practices and technologies that correlate with the characteristics of a place. Hence, a third space may lose its dynamism and ambiguity as meanings and practices are institutionalized in the name of a place. Yet other spaces of change and hybridity may also emerge as demographic changes alter the landscape of a particular place.

Although part of the responsibility for enacting curricular and pedagogical alternatives lies on the shoulders of educators, changing the practices of the city are just as important in this process. Federal, national, and state governmental bodies have tinkered toward school reform for more than a century (Kliebard, 1986; Tyack & Cuban, 1995). The findings of our study suggest that the knowledge and structural relations that comprise the broader city also need to be examined and altered if schools are to envision their students and practices differently. These distinctions are, in part, an effect of citywide structural relations and knowledge. As neighborhoods continue to be racially segregated, and as city officials and residents persist in discussing particular neighborhoods as safe (i.e., white and middle-class) and others as dangerous (i.e., black and Latina/o) spaces (Haymes, 1995), the continuity of this knowledge across space will prevail.

Conclusion

The concluding remarks of any book position its authors to define what might be done to ameliorate a particular problem. It is a position that we both embrace as well as one of which we are weary. We embrace the occasion to discuss what might be done to address the entangled issues of representation (i.e., knowledge), learning and democratic processes in schools. We particularly welcome the opportunity to discuss the tensions of schools as elements of larger configurations of social relations such as cities. However, the concluding section of any book is also an obligatory moment (i.e., historical and spatial) to more discourse about subjects and, in our case, institutions. It is a moment of power, specifically one of expert knowledge/power. It is an event to assert, or reassert, a new regime or knowledge and practice. We are unsure about this moment of prescription that suggests that a course of action will resolve the tensions at hand (Popkewitz, 1997).

The problem of the spatial (i.e., knowledge, technologies and practices) production of the East Side, West Side and Central City schools is a complicated one. One recommendation that seems readily transparent is broadening the number of discourses that circulate within the public spaces of the city, particularly within the media- and political-spaces. While we believe that this is a necessary move, we are not convinced that this has not already been the case. Alternative discourses already circulate within the city, especially among youth and particular community groups from the western part of the city. While alternative framings of these places surely do not have the institutional salience that other framings do, which is what our analysis identified in examining the Central City knowledge and practice, to negate their existence would be to misrepresent the complexity of the case.

Rather than highlight the existence and nature of alternative discourses, we believe that the city and its schools might be better served by discussing how power and knowledge are constituted through the injunction of systems of representation (i.e., discourse) and technologies. By positioning the realm of knowledge as an object of examination and critique, such discussions may help educators to identify how the widely accepted codes and knowledge of populations are socially constructed products, rather than timeless truths that correspond to the essential properties of being of groups of people. While this premise that individuals and populations are socially constructed is an argument that most academicians are familiar with (Rose, 1999), our findings suggest that this thesis has not found its way into the spaces of schools. Such discussions may be helpful with educators to broaden the realms of action and propel potentially disruptive practices. Yet, these conversations about the social constructed processes of populations need to position this knowledge of the subject and populations within the social coordination of objects, or what we have been referring to as space, rather than in the heads of educators.

The significance of discussing this knowledge as lying within spatial relations is premised on the fact that the tradition of examining educational reform and school knowledge has constructed teachers and principals as holders, or vessels, of professional and personal beliefs and ideologies that derail attempts at change (cf. Ravitch, 1983; Tyack & Cuban, 1995). The problem with this thesis is that even though beliefs may appear to change, the spatial relationships (i.e., knowledge, bodies, technologies, and apparatuses) of schools continue to propel particular bodily practices and activities. Hence, in reframing the problem as one of local knowledge, discussions with educators may now make the project of change one of identifying the wide range of relations that produce and maintain localized regimes of truth. The spatial boundaries of schools and school knowledge may be presented as perforated divides to show how the key propositions of the knowledge of the city and its subjects seep through these porous boundaries to find their way into educators' frameworks, and vice versa. These conversations have to take into consideration the centrifugal force of technologies. Educators (i.e., teachers, principals and educational researchers) cannot lose sight that layered technologies have an organizing element to them that structures new objects, knowledges and bodies so that they buttress and expand existing systems of reasoning. Educators need to understand how the introduction of new technologies does not necessarily mean alternative practices. There is always the chance, a very strong one at that, of the inscription of pre-existing meanings and the reproduction of practices. Discussions about the underlying discourses of student populations and those that underpin technologies may need to be built into conversations about change and alternatives.

The probability of re-inscription and reproduction does not mean that attempts at interrupting these relations of power should not be encouraged and pursued. When researchers and educators can jointly identify a few of the multitude of interconnected social relations that converge to produce an epistemology of teaching within "urban" schools, they multiply the points of entry for different kinds of action for educators, their students and researchers. The spaces (i.e., social relations) of media discourses, local political activities, and, of course, classroom practices can become important nodes of possibility for re-envisioning students, identifying their wants and assets, and realigning the logic of school and classroom practices. The caveat, however, is that attempts at disruption will require sophisticated and innovative modes, particularly since these relationships between school and city knowledge are enmeshed in overlapping projects of representation that appear seamless. We believe, though, that such interruptions are possible and necessary.

As an example, one such creative project initiated within a school-community sponsored project within Salt Valley City involved pairing a group of 18 local high school (14-18 year olds) and college students in a documentary arts project entitled "Across the Tracks: Voices from the West Side." This collaboration involved having the groups of students create short (i.e., 10-15 minute) films that deconstructed and unearthed the various meanings of the West Side space. The students and the instructor engaged in collaborative discussions that led to the identification of the various motifs of the different short films. One of them involved examining the media constructions of the West Side, particularly the racialized meanings within the city's newspapers and local television news productions. Meanwhile, another group of students explored the place making and sense of extended community that the diasporic Tongan residents had created on the western side of the city through church, park and commercial spaces. All of the films de-naturalized, one way or another, the premise of a one-dimensional space and group of people. Students and the facilitator explored how the various people who comprised the space termed the West Side had a plurality of aspirations, narratives and competencies that were rarely mentioned in official media reports, and that never surfaced within school knowledge. Learning and knowledge production became a process of moving outside of the school walls and exploring the various social relationships in which other meanings about populations and space were in circulation. This involved rearranging the existing school technologies (i.e., literacy pedagogies, instructional conversations) so that they were attuned to different ends and different subjects, that is, knowing and knowledge producing ones.

What is important about such projects and framings for educators and students is that they may be able to envision practices of possibility as lying around them within other contexts of relations (i.e., counter-narratives in the media, relations that subjugate the impacts of federal technologies), rather than within their belief systems or new technologies aiming to create more efficient modes of meeting particular population of students' needs. It was clear in the Central City data that teachers aligned themselves with somewhat different relations of power in representing themselves as not-West Side. They drew on readily available national discourses, technologies, and associations with other schools to organize their work. The possibilities for other educators within other parts of the city to reconceptualize their populations and themselves may also be possible. However, their ability to create and enact a third, or other, designation may be very difficult considering the institutionalization of discourses and technologies, as well as the investments by individuals across the city. If these other educators in Salt Valley District were to question how and under what spatial contexts communities and students of color mobilize other relations of power to self-define themselves in ways that do not correspond to those of institutional constructs, it might force educators to ask: How might we talk about and re-align ourselves differently in order to draw on communities of color's self-representations and rethink the categories of being that we continuously deploy?

A concluding remark pertaining to the emergence of third spaces within cities and their institutional structures, such as its schools, is that perturbations are potentially productive, or can be creatively productive, rather than reproductive of dominant power relations and knowledges. One outcome that such awareness may lead to is captured in the work of Elizabeth Moje and colleagues (2004) on the funds of knowledge and discourses across contexts including school, neighborhood, and peer groups:

> What is critical to our position is the sense that these spaces [community; institutional, including schools] can be reconstructed to form a third, different or alternative, space of knowledges and discourses. It is critical to examine not only knowledges and discourses themselves but also the funds in which knowledges and discourses are generated, because the funds help to make visible the social construction of knowledges and discourses. If the social nature of all funds—whether schools, communities, disciplines, popular culture, peer groups, or families—is not recognized, then the knowledges and discourses generated in each seem to take on a life of their own, as if they are somehow natural constructions that exist outside human interaction and relationships. (p. 45)

Awareness of the productive actions that hybrid third spaces entail may highlight for interlocutors in Salt Valley City and its schools possibilities for disrupting the binary that continues to place communities and students of color outside of the norm. Perhaps the notion of "natural" divisions along socio-spatial lines could be challenged, so that technologies, discourses, and knowledges could be examined for their roles in relations of power that shape the production of identity and practice.

Viewing social space, particularly a third space, as a "mix of opposition, unity, and contradiction which defines a socio-spatial dialectic" (Soja, 1989, p. 77) may help educators and city dwellers, as well as researchers, embrace the complexity of changing social and physical conditions. Such an approach may then lead to efforts to address explicitly what are shared commitments (e.g., successful learning and development of youth) in the face of contradictory forces that differentiate spaces from each other (e.g., funding and other technologies built on deficit-based definitions of particular communities; literacy curricula and clusters that reify historical, spatial, political divisions). We are not suggesting that a universal (i.e., raceless and classless) concept of the student be the goal, but argue that a fluid, multi-dimensional knowledge framework of the student and teacher be the objective.

However, we have to ask what is the role of intent, as well as the masking influence of school structures that hinder such awareness, or reflection, of what was previously unexamined and not understood? Do institutional workers, such as educators as well as city leaders, really want to see and change structures and processes that were central to current activity and that create and recreate social spaces? In Moje et al.'s (2004) work, teachers were committed to changing their practices in ways that embraced resources students brought to literacy learning. In school spaces, as we have shown, technologies, school and city discourses, historical and current race and class relations all mitigate against the production of hybrid third spaces. How might increasing understanding of relations of power, technologies, and knowledge motivate those in power to participate in the production of hybridity?

These questions about educators' intent and willingness are important transition points in our present discussion. These help us to reflexively identify the precarious terms and presuppositions of our own theorizing. As we indicated at the beginning of this section, the conclusions of books–particularly educational texts–position authors to define the next course of action. However, we realize that our discussion of possibilities and interruption are predicated on a theoretical discourse that can be located within the various philosophies of freedom, Marxist and Liberalist philosophical strands in particular (Popkewitz, 1997). What is important to realize about our own alignment within this body of writing is that it is an argument that has as its aspirations educational alternatives (i.e., discursive and structural) that might lead to individuals having fuller lives and a society that does not exclude them from participating in and altering the multitude of activities constituting what Antonio Gramsci (1971) termed political (i.e., State) and civil society.

Yet, we recognize that for educators to engage in work towards leveling the playing field caused by social inequities requires that they anchor, or affix, student identity. Theories of justice, equity and freedom necessitate that institutional workers name the not free as well as those not served justly. However, our central argument here is that these acts of identification involve a discursive act of symbolic violence (Derrida, 1998). That is, they dictate narrowing the subjectivities of individuals so that a recognizable individual or group is presented as a marginalized and subjugated constituent of state and macro-structural relations (Popkewitz, 1998B). Within the US, this has involved the construction of populations around racial, classed, gendered and migratory status designations (Foucault, 1991; Omi & Winant, 1991; Popkewitz, 1998A). The tension that exists within our theorizing involves destabilizing these very same networks of representation that educators have employed to rectify, in part, social disparities. While the aims drift from their ameliorative ends within city and school spaces at times (Tyack & Cuban, 1995), as well as are being laced with troubling discursive elements (see Anyon, 1997; McNeil, 2000), they are employed within schools, partly, to name and meet needs. Because institutions are charged with this task, the tension inherent in reductive knowledge and technologies may be unavoidable in societies where multi-nodal relations of self and social governmentality exist (Foucault, 1991; Rose, 1999).

Another undercurrent of our work and theorizing that needs to be scrutinized is the premise that our illumination of the ways that knowledge and technologies operate to construct populations and practices of difference will compel educators to want to reorient their field of relations to enact alternatives. Like most social research, an Enlightenment discourse of change is in operation here. The presupposition of this discourse is that once the truth is unveiled, people are going to act accordingly, or reasonably. The idea that educators are willing to question the knowledge frameworks and social relations that conjoin to make students and themselves identifiable once they know that these practices and identities are socially constructed may be doubtful. Our recommendation that educators rethink these relationships and knowledge may reflect an extreme naivety on our behalf. Educational practices are laden with educators' and institutions' investments. These practices allow them to act, identify and distinguish themselves professionally with some degree of certainty, a hallmark of modern institutions (Toulmin, 1992). For most educators in this study, the social relationship of knowledge and technologies has worked fine by their accounts. Only the Central City educators found themselves in a liminal space of knowledge and technologies. It may be likely that any attempt at turning the tide of educators' investments in these East Side and West Side constructs may be resisted with a great deal of resolve, regardless of how reasonable, or truthful, these findings may appear.

Finally, it needs to be remembered that the recommendations and conclusions that we have proffered in this chapter are themselves historical effects of spatial and temporal relations. Like many researchers (e.g., Behar, 1994; Lather & Smithies, 1997), we are concerned about the crystallization and subsequent redeployment of these findings and conclusions in new technologies of discipline on schools and educators. Readers need to keep in mind that regimes of truth involve each and every one of us–as nodal agents– and the ensuing coordination of technologies of institutionalization. Yet the importance of reflexive, critical work that attempts to unmask the workings of power is an enterprise that must be engaged in, even though it is fraught with tensions and unintentional outcomes.

APPENDIX

Research Methods

The District we studied serves approximately 25,000 students, and was experiencing an average annual growth rate in its population of students of color of 8 percent during the previous 5 years. Table 1 presents representative demographic data. This book presents results of our analyses of semi-structured interviews and reform documents from all 26 elementary schools in the district.

Table 1. Profile of schools in 2000-2001 academic year.

Number of schools	37 total: 26 elementary, 7 middle, 4 high schools
District ethnic/racial profile	Caucasian – 59% Hispanic – 26% Native American, African American Asian American, Pacific Islander – 2-5% each
Students receiving alternative language services	23%
Students receiving free and reduced lunch	51%

We designed this work as a case study, examining the District as one of the primary units of analysis. Given our theoretical framework that centers educators as active agents in the construction of social space, an interpretive approach was appropriate. Our primary data sources were identified as a way to provide us access to educators' perceptions, experiences, and practices.

Data Sources and Analytic Methods

Over 2 years, we conducted four sets of interviews with 60 teachers in focus groups and 20 administrators individually. The majority of the teachers and administrators were white and female—over ninety percent. The teachers were self-selected participants of each school's reform guidance committee. The interview questions that we asked focused on the characteristics of students, the needs of students, and the types of classroom practices employed, as well as the rationales for employing these practices. We asked about the relationship between these practices and how they related to defining and attending to their students' needs. We also asked about the distinctions, or differences, between East Side or West Side schools, particularly after seeing how these distinctions were drawn in the first set of focus group interviews. In pursuing this, we used specific school names (e.g., Lake View Elementary) to refer to these spaces—schools that the teachers themselves had indexed in making these distinctions—rather than the general terms of East Side or West Side. Our aim in asking these questions was to identify the knowledge, or discourse, that was summoned to name needs, practices, and purpose. Lastly, we prompted both teachers and administrators to identify the funding mechanisms, accountability measures, policies, and curricular programs that were part of the technologies, or relations, that aided them in identifying and meeting these needs.

Reform-mandated school improvement plans, mission statements, and grant applications were also collected. Our intent in collecting these was to examine what discourses were inscribed to define who students were, what they needed, as well as the school's and teachers' purpose/mission. Once it was evident to us that the East Side/West Side terms were salient constructs for teachers and administrators, with a connected set of propositions, we collected current and past newspaper articles that used these linguistic framings. The purpose of this activity was to determine whether a relationship existed between the discourses that were fixed in these media texts and the enunciative acts of school agents, as well as the nature of this relationship.

Definitions of constructs identified by the District as central to the reform effort (e.g., achievement, community involvement) were taken from District-level documents (e.g., original grant proposal to national foundation funding the reform, request for proposals to evaluate the project, guidelines for schools in producing their reform-mandated school improvement plans). To operationalize these constructs for use in qualitative coding of data, the 5 faculty members who made up the evaluation research team discussed the terms and District definitions, conducted initial coding of the same transcript both independently and together, and engaged in further discussion to reach a tentative consensus on definitions of codes. Four of the researchers then analyzed the same transcript independently and compared their results. Inconsistencies were discussed and final consensus reached on definitions and interpretations. Those four faculty then analyzed another transcript independently. We conducted an analysis of inter-rater reliability by first identifying the number of segments spoken by the interviewees (e.g., T1 speaks, then T3 speaks = two segments) and then tallying the number of agreements of coding of segments. Acceptable consistency (at least 70%) in coding for each construct was achieved after we coded the second transcript in common. We then coded the rest of the data independently, with pairs of researchers conducting constant comparative analysis (Lincoln & Guba, 1995) of the data with respect to a specific construct (e.g., accountability, teaching practices), identifying and explicating emergent codes and themes not included in the operationalized definitions, and each writing analytic memos (cf. Strauss & Corbin, 1998). Those memos and the pairs' coding were used to write final summaries of the pairs' work.

The next level of analysis relied upon critical discourse analysis (CDA) and elements of qualitative grounded theory. The two of us analyzed the summaries described above, as well as returning to interview transcripts and textual artifacts, using a CDA approach (Gee, 1999). We identified and tracked the syntactic structure and linguistic terms of the enunciations of teachers and administrators. We identified the knowledge propositions that were invoked about practice, self, and student by their language. These discursive framings were juxtaposed to the syntactic and linguistic structure of other texts in order to determine the saliency and the dispersion of this knowledge—first the textual transcriptions of other interviews, and then to the framings of East Side/West Side presented in the media texts. We determined points of convergence and divergence amidst the different social relations, and examined the data for negative exemplars and alternative explanations.

Limitations in the data include that we interviewed 4-6 teachers per school and those teachers were nominated by their principals or self-selected, rather than the whole faculty being invited to inform our work. The participating teachers' views may not have been representative of their schools. In addition, reform-mandated documents were crafted in response to District-developed guidelines, and may have not captured broader school practices. Still, we built relationships with schools over 2 years, interviewing many of the same teachers and principals over that time period, so that the trust we achieved may have ameliorated some of the issues of breadth versus depth, and access to the full range of school practices related to advocacy.

Transcription Conventions

The transcripts bear conventions that denote intonation of the speakers. The following symbols represent the intonations and gestures:

Italics	speaker's emphasis on word
[ ]	Interconnected, or simultaneous, speech in a dialogue
:	Extra colon indicates longer elongation
/	Half second of silence

REFERENCES

Ahlstrand, Elisabeth, Carlsson, Gorel, Hartman, Sven G., Magnusson, Lars, & Rannstrom, Annika (1996). Teacher knowledge development in a social and individual context. In M. Kompf, W.R. Bond, D. Dworet & R. T. Boak (Eds.), *Changing research and practice: Teachers' professionalism, identities and knowledge* (pp. 186—210). London: Falmer Press.

Althusser, Louis (1971). *Lenin and philosophy, and other essays*. New York: Monthly Review Press.

Anderson, Benedict (2000). *Imagined communities: Reflections on the origin and spread of nationalism*. London: Verso Editions.

Anderson, James D. (1988). *The education of blacks in the South, 1860-1935*. Chapel Hill, NC: University of North Carolina Press.

Anyon, Jean (1997). *Ghetto schooling: A political economy of urban educational reform*. New York: Teachers College Press.

Anzaldua, Gloria (1987). *Borderlands: The new Mestiza*. San Francisco, CA: Spinsters/Aunt Lute.

Ares, Nancy & Buendía (Forthcoming). Advocacy in school reform: Local translations of national conversations. *Teachers College Record*.

Arrington, Leonard, J. & Bitton, Davis (1979). *The Mormon Experience: A history of the Latter Day Saints*. New York: Random House.

Bahktin, Michale M. (1986). *Speech genres and other essays* (M. Holquist, Trans.). Austin, Texas: University of Texas Press.

Baird, John (2000). Across the great divide. *The Salt Lake Tribune*. 5/21/2000. A1.

Baltezore, Jay (1996). When junk starts piling up in the yard, property values start going down. *The Salt Lake Tribune*. 1/15/1996. D3.

Behar, Ruth (1994). *Translated woman: Crossing the border with Esperanza's story*. Boston: Beacon Press.

Berger, John (1972). *Ways of seeing*. London: British Broadcasting Corporation and Penguin Books

Bhabha, Homi (1994). *The location of culture*. New York: Routledge.

Borman, Kenneth & Spring, Joel H. (1984). *Schools in central cities: Structure and process*. New York: Longman.

Bourdieu, Pierre (1990). *The logic of practice*. Stanford, CA: Stanford Press.

Boyer, Christine M. (1990). The return of aesthetics to city planning. In Dennis Cross (Ed.), *Philosophical streets: New approaches to urbanism* (pp. 160—185). Washington D.C.: Maisonneuve Press.

Boyer, Christine M. (1986). *Dreaming the rational city*. Cambridge, MA: The MIT Press.

Buendía, Edward (2002). Enveloping pedagogies: The codification of instructional technologies. *Pedagogy, Culture and Society, 10*(3), 387—409.

Buendía, Edward (2000). Power and possibility: The construction of a pedagogical practice. *Teaching and Teacher Education, 16*(2), 147—163.

Bullough, Robert V. & Gitlin, Andrew D. (2001). *Becoming a student of teaching*. New York: Routledge Press.

Butler, Judith (1999). *Gender trouble: Feminism and the inversion of identity*. New York: Routledge.

Carew, George (1997). Liberalism and the politics of emancipation. In L. R. Gordon (Ed.), *Existence in black: An anthology of Black Existential philosophy* (pp. 225-241). New York: Routledge.

Castells, Manuel (2000). *The rise of the network society* (Second Edition). Malden, MA: Blackwell Publishers.

Cetina, Karin K. (1999). *Epistemic cultures: How the sciences make knowledge*. Cambridge, MA: Harvard University Press.

Clark, Andy (1997). *Being there: Putting brain, body and world together again*. Cambridge MA: MIT Press.

Coleman, Ronald G. (1980). *A history of blacks in Utah: 1825-1910*. Unpublished doctoral dissertation, University of Utah.

Collins, Patricia H. (1991). *Black feminist thought*. New York: Routledge.

Defa, Dennis R. (2000). The Goshute Indians of Utah. In F.S. Cuch (Ed.), *A history of Utah's American Indians* (pp. 73-122). Salt Lake City, UT: Utah State Divison of Indians Affairs and the Utah State Division of History.

Delanty, Gerard (2000). *Modernity and postmodernity: Knowledge, power and the self*. Thousand Oaks, CA: Sage Press.

Delgado Bernal, Dolores (1998). Using a Chicana Feminist Epistemology in Educational Research. *Harvard Educational Review, 68*(4), 555-582.

Delpit, Lisa (1996). *Other people's children: Cultural conflict in the classroom*. New York: New Press.

Denzin, Norman K. (1997). *Interpretive ethnography: Ethnographic practices for the 21st century*. Thousand Oaks, CA: Sage.

Derrida, Jacques (1998). *Monolingualism of the other; Or, the prosthesis of origin* (Trans: Patrick Mensah). Stanford, CA: Stanford Press.

Dolby, Nadine (2001). *Constructing racialized selves: Youth, identity and popular culture in South Africa*. Albany, New York: State University of New York Press.

Drake, St. Clair & Horace, Clayton R. (1970). *The black metropolis: A study of Negro life in a northen city*. New York: Harcourt, Brace.

Eckert, Percy (1989). *Jocks and burnouts: Social categories and identity in the high school*. New York: Teachers College Press.

Edsall, Thomas B. & Edsall, Mary D. (1992). *Chain reaction: The impact of race, rights and taxes on American politics*. New York: W.W. Norton and Co.

Fairclough, Norman (1995). *Media discourse*. New York: E. Arnold Press.

Fine, Michelle (1995). Working the hyphens: Reinventing self and other qualitative research. In N. Denzin & Y. Lincoln (Eds.), *The qualitative research handbook, Vol. 2* (pp. 70—82). Thousand Oaks, CA: Sage Press.

Fine, Michelle (1991). *Framing dropouts: Notes on the politics of an urban high school*. Albany, NY: State University of New York Press.

Foucault, Michel (1991). Governmentality. In G. Burchell, C. Gordon, & P. Miller (Eds.), *The Foucault effect: Studies in governmentality* (pp. 87—104). Chicago, IL: University of Chicago Press.

Foucault, Michel (1988). The ethic of care for the self as a practice of freedom. In J. Bernauer & D. Rasmussen, (Eds.), *The Final Foucault* (pp. 1-20). Cambridge, MA: MIT Press.

Foucault, Michel (1980). Truth and power. In M. Foucault, *Power/Knowledge: Selected interviews and other writings 1972-1977* (pp. 109—133). New York: Pantheon Books.

Foucault, Michel (1978). *History of sexuality, Vol. I*. New York: Pantheon Books.

Foucault, Michel (1977). *Discipline and punish: The birth of the prison*. London: Allen Lane.

Foucault, Michel (1972) *Archeology of knowledge*. New York: Pantheon Books.

Fraser, Nancy (1991). *Unruly practices: Power, discourse, and gender in contemporary social theory.* Minneapolis: University of Minnesota Press.

Gee, James P. (1999). *An introduction to discourse analysis: Theory and method.* New York: Routledge.

Gitlin, Andrew, Buendía, E., Crosland, K., & Doumbia, F. (2003). The production of margin and center: Welcoming-unwelcoming of immigrant students. *American Educational Research Journal, 40*(1), 91-122.

Gonzalez, Norma, Andrade, Rosi, Civil, Marta, & Moll, Luis (2001). Bridging funds of distributed knowledge: Creating zones of practices in mathematics. *Journal of Education for Students Placed at Risk, JESPAR; 6*(1-2), 115-32.

Gramsci, Antonio (1971). *Selections from the prison notebooks.* London: International Publishers.

Hacking, Ian (1992). *The social construction of what?* Cambridge, MA: Harvard University Press.

Hall, Stuart (1997). Representation. In S. Hall (Ed.), *Representation: Cultural representations and signifying practices*, pp. 13-74. London: Sage.

Haney, Walt (2000). The myth of the Texas miracle in education. *Education Policy Analysis Archives 8*(41), http://epaa.asu.edu/epaa/v8n41.

Haraway, Donna J. (1991). *Simians, cyborgs, and women: The reinvention of nature.* New York: Routledge Press.

Haymes, Stephan N. (1995). *Race, culture and the city: A pedagogy for black urban struggle.* Albany, NY: State University of New York Press.

Hooks, Bell (1990). *Yearning: Race, gender, and cultural politics.* Boston, MA: South End Press.

Huckin, Thomas (1995). Critical discourse analysis. *The Journal of TESOL-France, 2*(7), 95-110.

Jackson, Kenneth T. (1985). *Crabgrass frontier: The suburbanization of the United States.* New York: Oxford University Press.

Jacobs, Gregory S. (1998). *Getting around Brown: Desegregation, development and the Columbus public schools.* Ohio State University Press.

Jones, LeAlan & Newman, Lloyd (1997). *Our America: Life and death on the South Side of Chicago.* New York: Scribner Press.

Kantor, Harvey (2004). *Notes on race, class, space, and the organization of schooling in Salt Lake City, 1960-1990.* Unpublished manuscript.

Kantor, Harvey A. (1988). *Learning to earn: School, work, and vocational reform in California, 1880-1930*. Madison, WI: University of Wisconsin Press.

Kantor, Harvey A. & Brenzel, Barbara (1993). Urban education and the "truly disadvantaged": The historical roots of the contemporary crisis, 1945-1990. In M. B. Katz (Ed.), *The "underclass" debate: Views from history* (pp. 367-402). Princeton, NJ: Princeton University Press.

Kennedy, Randall (2002). *Nigger: The strange career of a troublesome word*. New York: Pantheon Books.

Kliebard, Herbert M. (1986). *The struggle for the American curriculum 1893-1958*. New York: Routledge Press.

Kozol, Jonathon (1994). *Savage inequalities: Children in America's schools*. New York: Perrenial.

Kuhn, Thomas S. (1970). *The structure of scientific revolutions*. Chicago: University of Chicago Press.

Lather, Patti & Smithies, Chris. (1997). *Troubling the angles: Women living with HIV/AIDS*. Boulder, CO: Westview Press.

Latour, Bruno & Woolgar, Steve (1979). *Laboratory life: The social construction of scientific facts*. Beverly Hills, CA: Sage Publications.

Lee, Stacy J. (1996). *Unraveling the "model minority" stereotype*. New York: Teachers College Press.

Lefebvre, Henri (1991). *The production of space*. UK: Blackwell.

Lincoln, Yvonna S. & Guba, Egon G. (1995). *Naturalistic inquiry*. Thousand Oaks: Sage Publications.

Lipman, Pauline (2002). Making the global city, making inequality: The political economy and cultural politics of Chicago school policy. *American Educational Research Journal, 39*(2), 379-419.

Loomis, Barry (2000). Westside anger: Community council leader saw mall as bulwark against 'Spanish stuff.' *The Salt Lake Tribune*. 7/29/2000. A1 & A3.

Lyotard, Jean-Francios (1984). *The postmodern condition: A report on knowledge*. Minneapolis: University of Minnesota Press.

MacCannell, Dean (1989). *The tourist: A theory of the leisure class*. New York: Schocken Books.

Massey, Douglas S. & Denton, Nancy A. (1993). *American apartheid: Segregation and the making of the underclass*. Cambridge, MA: Harvard University Press.

May, Dean L. (1987). *Utah: A people's history*. Salt Lake City, UT: University of Utah Press.

McCarthy, Cameron (1998). *The uses of culture: Education and the limits of ethnic affiliation*. New York: Routledge Press.

McCarthy, Cameron & Crichlow, Warren (1993). Theories of identity, theories of representation, theories of race. In C. McCarthy and W. Crichlow (Eds.), *Race, identity and representation in education* (pp. xiii—xxix). New York: Routledge.

McCarthy, Cameron, Rodriguez, Alicia, Buendía, Edward, Meacham, Shuaib, David, Stephan, Wilson-Brown, Carrie, Godina, Heriberto (1997). Race, suburban resentment and the representation of the inner city in contemporary film and television. *Cultural Studies, 1*, 121—140.

McCormick, John S. (2000). *The gathering place: An illustrated history of Salt Lake City*. Salt Lake City, UT: Signature Books.

McDermott, Ray (1996). The acquisition of a child by a learning disability. In. S. Chaiklin & J. Lave, *Understanding practice: Perspectives on activity and context* (pp. 269-305). Cambridge, UK: Cambridge University Press.

McIntyre, Alice (1997). *Making meaning of whiteness: Exploring racial identity with white teachers*. Albany, New York: State University of New York Press.

McIntyre, Elaine, Rosebery, Ann, & Gonzalez, Norma (2001). *Classroom Diversity: Connecting curriculum to children's lives*. Westport, CT: Heinemann.

McKay, Sandra & Wong, Sau-Ling Cynthia (1996). Multiple discourses multiple identities investment and agency in second-language learning among Chinese adolescent immigrant students. *Harvard Educational Review, 66*, 577—608.

McLaren, Peter & Farahmandpur, Ramin (2000). Reconsidering Marx in post-Marxist times: A requiem for postmodernism? *Educational Researcher, 29*(3), 25—33.

McNeil, Linda (2000). *Contradictions of school reform: Educational costs of standardized testing*. New York: Routledge.

McNeil, Linda (1987). *Contradictions of control: School structure and school knowledge*. New York: Routledge.

McNeil, Linda & Valenzuela, Angela (1998). *The harmful impact of TASS system of testing in Texas: Beneath the accountability rhetoric*. Cambridge, MA: The Civil Rights Project, Harvard University.

McPherson, Robert S. (2000). Setting the stage: Native America revisited. In F.S. Cuch (Ed.), *A history of Utah's American Indians* (pp. 3—24). Salt Lake City, UT: Utah State Divison of Indians Affairs and the Utah State Division of History.

Menchaca, Martha (1997). Early racist discourses: The roots of deficit thinking. In R.R. Valencia (Ed.), *The evolution of deficit thinking: Educational thought and practice* (pp. 13—40). Washington, DC: Falmer Press.

Meyer, Stephan G. (2000). *As long as they don't move next door: Segregation and racial conflict in American neighborhoods.* New York: Rowman & Littlefield Publishers.

Moje, Elizabeth, Ciechanowski, Kathryn, M., Kramer, Katherine (2004). Working toward third space in content area literacy. *Reading Research Quarterly, 39*(1), 38—70.

Morantz, Allison (1996). Desegregation at risk: Threat and reaffirmation in Charlotte. In G. Orfield, S.E. Eaton, Harvard Civil Rights Project on School Desegregation (Eds.), *Dismantling desegregation: The quiet reversal of Brown v. Board of Education* (pp. 179-206). New York: The New Press.

Moriyasu, Haruko T. (1996). Salt Lake's Nihonjin Machi. In T. Negata (Ed.), *Japanese Americans in Utah* (pp. 38—45). Salt Lake City, UT: JA Centennial Committee.

Morrison, Toni (1992). *Playing in the dark.* Cambridge: Harvard University Press.

Neckerman, Kathryn M. & Wilson, William J. (1988). Schools and poor communities. Council of Chief State School Officers (Ed.), *School success for students at risk* (pp. 28—47). Orlando, FL: Harcourt Brace Jovanovick.

Nichols, Jeffrey D. (2002). *Prostitution, polygamy, and power: Salt Lake City, 1847-1918.* Urbana, IL: University of Illinois Press.

Noguera, Pedro A. (2003). *City schools and the American dream.* New York: Teachers College Press.

Oakes, Jeanie (1985). *Keeping track: How schools structure inequality.* New Haven, CT: Yale University Press.

Olsen, Laurie (1997). *Made in America.* New York: New Press.

Omi, Michael & Winant, Howard (1994). *Racial formation in the United States: From the 1960s to the 1990s.* New York: Routledge.

Orfield, Gary (2001). *Schools more separate: Consequences of a decade of resegregation* (Report No. UD034308). Cambridge, MA: Harvard Civil Rights Project. (ERIC Document Reproduction Service No. ED459217)

Orfield, Gary (1996). Turning back to segregation. In G. Orfield, S.E. Eaton and the Harvard Project on School Desegregation, *Dismantling desegregation* (pp. 1—22. New York: New Press.

Papanikilas, Helen, Z (1976). *The peoples of Utah*. Salt Lake City, UT: Utah State Historical Society.

Park, Robert, E. (1925). *The city*. Chicago: University of Chicago Press.

Parker, Laurence (2003). Critical race theory and its implications for methodology and policy analysis in higher education desegregation. In G.R. Lopez, & L. Parker (Eds.), *Interrogating racism in qualitative research methodology*. New York: Peter Lang.

Perea, Juan (1997). *Immigrants out! The new nativism and the anti-immigrant impulse in the United States*. New York: New York University Press.

Popkewitz, Thomas S. (1998A). The sociology of knowledge and the sociology of education: Michel Foucault and critical traditions. In C.A. Torres and T.R. Mitchell (Eds.), *Sociology of Education: Emerging perspectives* (pp. 47—90). Albany, NY: State University of New York Press.

Popkewitz, Thomas S. (1998B). *Struggling for the soul: The politics of schooling and the construction of the teacher*. New York: Teachers College Press.

Popkewitz, Thomas S. (1997). A changing terrain of knowledge and power: A social epistemology of educational research. *Educational Researcher*, 26(9), 18—29.

Ravitch, Diane (1983). *The troubled crusade: American education 1945-1980*. New York: Basic Books.

Rist, Ray (1973). *The urban school*. Cambridge, MA: MIT Press.

Rodman, Margaret C. (2003). Empowering place: Multilocality and multivocality. In S. M. Lowe & D. Lawrence-Zúñiga (Eds.), *The anthropology of space and place: Locating culture* (pp. 204—223). Malden, MA: Blackwell Publishing.

Roediger, David (1991). *The wages of whiteness: Race and the making of the American working class*. New York: Routledge Press.

Rosaldo, Renato (1989). *Culture and truth: The remaking of social analysis*. Boston, MA: Beacon Press.

Rose, Nicholas (1999). *Governing the soul: The shaping of the private self.* London: Free Association Books.

Rose, Nicholas (1996). *Inventing our selves: Psychology, power, and personhood.* New York: Cambridge University Press.

Salt Lake Evening Telegram (1907). *The Salt Lake Evening Telegram.* 11/22/1907. For Sale, Beautiful on east side

Sanjek, Roger (1998). *The future of us all: Race and neighborhood politics in New York City.* Ithaca, NY: Cornell University Press.

Shaw, Clifford & MacKay, Henry D. (1931). *Social factors in juvenile delinquency: Report on the causes of crime, 2*(60). Washington, D.C.: National Commission of Law Observance and Enforcement.

Shields, Robert (1997). Spatial stress and resistance: Social meanings of spatialization. In G. Benko & U. Strohmayer (Eds.), *Space and social theory* (pp. 186—202). Malden, MA: Blackwell Publishers.

Slater, Dennis (1997). Geopolitics and the postmodern: Issues of knowledge, difference, and North-South relations. In G. Benko & U. Strohmayer (Eds.), *Space and social theory* (pp. 324—335). Malden, MA: Blackwell Publishers

Soja, Edward (1996). *Thirdspace: Journeys to Los Angeles and other real-and-imagined places.* Cambridge, MA: Blackwell Press.

Soja, Edward (1989). *Postmodern geographies: The reassertion of space in critical social theory.* London: Verso.

Solomon, Patrick R. (1992). *Black resistance in high school: Forging a separatist culture.* Albany, NY: State University of New York Press.

Strauss, Anselm & Corbin, Juliet M. (1998). *Basics of qualitative research: Techniques and procedures for developing grounded theory*, Second Edition. London: Sage.

Takaki, Ronald (1994). *A different mirror: A history of multicultural America.* San Francisco: Back Bay Books.

Timmerman, Maria A. (2004). The influences of three interventions on prospective elementary teachers' beliefs about knowledge base needed for teaching mathematics. *School Science and Mathematics, 104*(8), 369—383.

Toulmin, Stephan (1992). *Cosmopolis: The hidden agenda of modernity.* Chicago, IL: University of Chicago Press.

Toulmin, Stephan E. (1972). *Human understanding.* Princeton, NJ: Princeton University Press.

Tuttle, Robert (2000, September 7). West side story, part II: Population growth has shifted from East to West, meaning big changes for a once ignored community. *Salt Lake City Weekly* (pp. 18—20, 22—23).

Tyack, David, & Cuban, Larry (1995). *Tinkering toward utopia: A century of public school reform*. Cambridge, MA: Harvard University Press.

U.S. Census Bureau (2003). *Utah 2000: Summary social, economic and housing characteristics*. Washington, DC: U.S. Census Bureau.

U.S. Government (2001). *Leave No Child Behind Act of 2001*. Washington, DC: The National Clearinghouse for Bilingual Education.

Utah Office of Planning and Budget (1989). *Utah demographic report*. Salt Lake City, Utah: Demographic & Economic Analysis, Utah Office of Planning & Budget.

Valdés, Guadalupe (2001). *Learning and not learning English: Latino students in American schools*. New York: Teachers College Press.

Valencia, Richard R. (1997). Conceptualizing the notion of deficit thinking. In R.R. Valencia (Ed), *The evolution of deficit thinking: Educational thought and practice* (pp. 1—12). Washington, DC: Falmer Press.

Valenzuela, Angela (2003). High stakes testing in Texas. Keynote address, *American Educational Studies Association*, Mexico City, Mexico.

Valenzuela, Angela (1999). *Subtractive schooling*. Ithaca, NY: State University of New York Press.

Villenas, Sophia (1996). The colonizer/colonized. *Harvard Educational Review, 66*, 711—731.

Vogel, Dan (1986). *Indian's origins and the Book of Mormon*. Salt Lake City, UT: Signature Books.

Ward, David (1989). *Poverty, ethnicity, and the American city: Changing conceptions of the slum and the ghetto*. Cambridge, UK: Cambridge University Press.

Ward, Stephen V. (1998). *Selling places: The marketing and promotion of towns and cities 1850-2000*. New York: Routledge.

White, Alan R. (1982). *The nature of knowledge*. Totowa, NJ: Rowman and Littlefield.

Williams, Raymond (1977). *Marxism and literature*. Oxford: Oxford University Press.

Wilson, David (1996). Metaphors, growth coalitions, and black poverty neighborhoods in a U.S. city. *Antipode, 28*(1), 72—97.

Wilson, William J. (1987). *The truly disadvantaged: The inner city, the underclass, and public policy*. Chicago: University of Chicago Press.

INDEX

academics, 82
accountability, 22-23,
aesthetic caring, 22
alternative pedagogies, 105
African-Americans, 17-20, 48
Althusser, Louis, 33
American Party, 52
Anyon, Jean, 13
at risk, 83, 84, 87
Book of Mormon, 47
Boyer, Christine, 14
Bransford, John S., 51
brothels, 51-52
Brown vs. Topeka, 18
Brown, William Thurston, 51
built environment, 94
   historical and contemporary systems of representation, 103
Central City, 77, 78
   contestation, 105
   contested space, 79
   relations of power, 109
Chicago, 20
Chicago Public School, 23
Chinese, 48
city segmentation, 14, 50
city segregation, 12-13, 92, 100-101
   banking industry, 15, 18, 101
   freeways, 47
   media, 55-56
   politics, 16
   racial segregation, 12
   railroads, 47, 48-49
   realtors, 54
   schools, 20
collective school identity, 75
Columbus, Ohio, 18
compensatory programs, 100
curricular and pedagogical alternatives, 105-106
   citywide structural relations, 106
   governmental bodies, 106
Denton, Nancy, 13
desegregation, 19
Deseret News, 53
desirable/undesirable spaces, 49
Detroit, 20
differentiated curricula & practices, 20-22, 24, 97
   defensive pedagogy, 22
discourse, 2, 5, 26
   ambiguity, 77-79
   binary logic, 63
   color blind, 98
   disadvantaged, the
   hybridity, 78, 81, 91
   institutionally specific spatial relations, 96
   production, 58
   knowledge and power, 37
   "Other," 47
   scientific discourse, 16-17
   silence, 80
durability of educational practices, 95
East Side
   discourse, 56, 65-66

indexical usage, 67-68
ontology, 65-66
socio-economic status, 54
east/west binary, 79, 80
  disjuncture, 105
Elmhurst-Corona, New York, 15
Evening Telegram, 50
Foucault, Michel, 1, 3, 6, 8, 13
Fremonts, 47
gentrification, 14
ghetto, 17
Goshutes, 47
Greek immigrants, 48-49, 52
Haymes, Stephen, 17
high status knowledge, 21
Hill, Joe, 51
hypersegregation, 13-14, 97
ideology, 32
immigrants, 77
inner city, 12-14, 83, 84, 85, 86, 90
inner city student, 25-26
intent
  relations of power, 111
International Baccalaureate, 23
Jackson, Kenneth, 18
Jacobs, Gregory, 18
Japanese-Americans, 49
Kantor, Harvey, 20
Kennedy, Randal, 45
knowledge, 4-5
  and ideology, 32, 35
  discourse, 37
  differentiated spaces, 98
  examination and critique, 107
  Logical Positivism, 30
  modernist, 29

productive and reproductive, 95
postmodernism, 32
see discourse
spatial differentiation, 98
spatial productions, 98
Kuhn, Thomas, 30
Lefebvre, Henri, 6, 38
Lipman, Pauline, 23
literacy programs, 72-75, 79, 86, 88, 90
  enriched, compensatory, 101
local knowledge, 92
  durability, 92
  durability, naturalness, 102
  historical racial and class
    representations, 94
Logical Positivism, 30
Los Angeles, 20
MacKay, Henry, 16
magnet high schools, 23
Massey, Douglas, 13
Marx, Karl, 32
math and science academies, 24
McCarthy, Cameron, 26
McCormick, John, 52
McNeil, Linda, 22
  defensive pedagogy, 22
Mexican Americans/Chicanos, 21-23
Meyer, Stephan, 13
Mormons, 47
New York City, 12, 15
Nihonjin Machi, 49
No Child Left Behind Act, 70
nostalgia, 79, 82, 84, 85, 91
Oakes, Jeannie, 21
Orfield, Gary, 20

Index

Paiutes, 47
Park, Robert, 16
   zones of blight, 17
politics of race, 97
Popkewitz, Thomas, 25
post-industrialization, 13
practices, 36-39
   and discourse, 37
   and technologies, 37
   production of knowledge, 36
   spatial, 38, 49
race relations, 98
   individualism, 98
racial invisibility, 65-66
racial segregation, 12-16
relations of power, 18
   interrupting, 18
re-segregated schools, 96
resistance, 79, 82, 91
Rose, Nicholas, 3, 37
Salt Valley City, 46-50
   business district, 50
   segregation, 51-54
   Plum Alley, 51-52
Sanjek, Roger, 15
school clusters, 86, 89
school improvement plans, 86, 88
segregated schools, 20-24
   representation, 26
Shaw, Clifford, 16
Shoshone, 47
slums, 16-17
social services, 80, 82, 83, 88
social space, 12, 78, 79, 80, 81, 91
   representation, 16- 20
Socialists, 51
sociology of knowledge, 3

Soja, Edward, 6, 28, 38
Solomon, Patrick, 26
space, 11
   geographical divisions, 100
   production of, 38
   technologies, 39
spaces of freedom, 105
   alternative knowledge frameworks, 105
spatial
   categories, 95
   differentiation, 107
   color- and class-blind, 95
   relations, 3, 12-15, 90
spatial knowledge, 92
   built environments, 103
   constructed nature, 104
spatial metaphors, 97
spatial production, 107
   alternatives discourses, 107
   discussions with educators, 108
spatialization, 72-75, 84, 103
   discursive divisions, 104
spatialize, 38, 87-99
   shorthand constructs, 98
   professional identities, 104
spatializing, 38, 77-99
structural relations, 24
suburbs, 13-16
symbolic language for the politics of race, 16-18
   codes, 18
symbolic violence, 21
teacher attitudes, 22-23
technologies, 69, 77, 78, 80, 81, 83, 88, 89, 90
Texas Assessment of Academic Skills, 23

third spaces, 110
   productive actions, 110
Thirdspace, 42
Toulmin, Stephen, 30
tracking, 21
trialectic, 28, 37, 42, 44
Unitarian Church, 51
urban student, 18-19, 25-26
Utes, 47
Valenzuela, Angela, 22, 23, 26
West Side
   deconstructed, 109
   discourse, 52-53, 55, 59-62
   educators, 61
   history, 51-56
   indexical usage, 63-65
   ontology, 60
   space, 64
   structural relations, 53-54
   technologies, 70-73
whiteness, 104

Intersections in Communications and Culture

Global Approaches and Transdisciplinary Perspectives

General Editors: Cameron McCarthy & Angharad N. Valdivia

An Institute of Communications Research, University of Illinois Commemorative Series

This series aims to publish a range of new critical scholarship that seeks to engage and transcend the disciplinary isolationism and genre confinement that now characterizes so much of contemporary research in communication studies and related fields. The editors are particularly interested in manuscripts that address the broad intersections, movement, and hybrid trajectories that currently define the encounters between human groups in modern institutions and societies and the way these dynamic intersections are coded and represented in contemporary popular cultural forms and in the organization of knowledge. Works that emphasize methodological nuance, texture and dialogue across traditions and disciplines (communications, feminist studies, area and ethnic studies, arts, humanities, sciences, education, philosophy, etc.) and that engage the dynamics of variation, diversity and discontinuity in the local and international settings are strongly encouraged.

LIST OF TOPICS

- Multidisciplinary Media Studies
- Cultural Studies
- Gender, Race, & Class
- Postcolonialism
- Globalization
- Diaspora Studies
- Border Studies
- Popular Culture
- Art & Representation
- Body Politics
- Governing Practices
- Histories of the Present
- Health (Policy) Studies
- Space and Identity
- (Im)migration
- Global Ethnographies
- Public Intellectuals
- World Music
- Virtual Identity Studies
- Queer Theory
- Critical Multiculturalism

Manuscripts should be sent to:

Cameron McCarthy OR **Angharad N. Valdivia**
Institute of Communications Research
University of Illinois at Urbana-Champaign
222B Armory Bldg., 555 E. Armory Avenue
Champaign, IL 61820

To order other books in this series, please contact our Customer Service Department:
(800) 770-LANG (within the U.S.)
(212) 647-7706 (outside the U.S.)
(212) 647-7707 FAX

Or browse online by series:
www.peterlang.com